YOUR FLOURISHING BRAIN

HOW TO REBOOT YOUR BRAIN
AND LIVE YOUR BEST LIFE NOW

BY BOB HOFFMAN, DC
AND PATRICK K PORTER, PhD

"Take up one idea. Make that one idea your life - think of it, dream of it, live on that idea. Let the brain, muscles, nerves, every part of your body, be full of that idea, and just leave every other idea alone. This is the way to success."

Swami Vivekananda

Patrick K. Porter, Ph.D.
Brain Wellness Unlimited
1822-6 South Glenburnie Road
PMB 362
New Bern, NC 28562

For more information on where Dr. Porter will be leading workshops in your area go to www.self-masterytechnology.com and become a part of the awakening of a planet...You could be the person who changes our world's thinking forever!

ISBN: 9781937111267

"I do not think there is any thrill that can go through the human heart like that felt by the inventor as he sees some creation of the brain unfolding to success... such emotions make a man forget food, sleep, friends, love, everything."

Nikola Tesla

TABLE OF CONTENTS

"I think the brain is essentially a computer and consciousness is like a computer program. It will cease to run when the computer is turned off. Theoretically, it could be re-created on a neural network, but that would be very difficult, as it would require all one's memories."

Stephen Hawking

FOREWORD

Evolution isn't about the changing of one life form to another. Evolution is about the ability to survive when the environment around you is changing. It's about the ability to adapt, to modify your actions to better suit the needs of the changing climate. When you are caught in the moment to moment challenge of business, personal issues, financial crises and/or emotional distractions, your ability to recognize the need to change is often impaired. So it goes in the practice of Chiropractic.

As we look at Chiropractic today it becomes self-evident that this once vibrant profession is in trouble. Incomes have fallen, the number of people seeking Chiropractic care has dropped, and we are seeing offices close. This field, which was once the leader in alternative health care, is today seldom ever mentioned in that group.

The origins of Chiropractic produced some theories about health and healing that were controversial yet produced results that were amazing. Those results have been keeping the profession alive in spite of great opposition from both outside and inside the profession. These results are not just about the relief of pain but tell about incredible recoveries from illness's and life challenges that usually end in tragedy.

The influence of health insurance has had a devastating effect on the profession. It has created a shift in the intent of Chiropractic care from the original concept of improved nervous system function, albeit a somewhat challengeable theory of nerve root compression, to a medical model of diagnosis for billing purposes. While this may sound reasonable, it has had a profound effect on the intent of care. The medical model is built on symptom relief, not improved neurological function. As medical costs continue to increase, the insurance money is less available for care outside of medicine. The Chiropractic profession is now caught between a rock and a hard spot because we are losing income due to decreased insurance payments and coverage, combined with a public that only sees us as a pain relief health care service. Add to that the fact that we have not updated our knowledge about the cause of vertebral subluxation or "why" the adjustment achieves such incredible results, and further recognize that many other professions have entered into the pain relief field, and you now have a disaster in process. There is an old saying about investments, "You will get a diminishing return on your investment as the market becomes saturated" which holds true in light of the profession situation. With all this in mind it is past time for us to revisit the direction of the profession.

Chiropractic is the only health field which has not altered its basic understanding or approach. Medicine has gone through several dramatic shifts as has Dentistry. The time has come for Chiropractic to update! Today the time for a new understanding of the power behind Chiropractic has arrived. This is the real secret of Chiropractic!

However, change calls for great leadership. It takes courage, commitment and dedication to step out of the old comfortable traditions to bring about a new direction for this profession. The work being done in the field of neuroscience outside the profession has provided the opportunity to revisit our basic concepts and understanding of "How" and "Why" Chiropractic continues to produce great results.

While we are aware of the concepts of positive thinking and affirmations, today technology is playing a powerful role in bringing this to life. The techniques of self-mastery now include direct brain training and instrumentation to augment the experience. Drs. Hoffman and Porter are leaders in this new approach. It has been my pleasure to work with both of these gentlemen in the development of this new direction for Chiropractic. The evolution of the profession is well under way. The option for change has passed. This book is about the future - your future and the future of the profession

- Dr. Richard Barwell, D.C.

CHAPTER
ONE

Why Do We Need Brain-Based Wellness?

Why Do We Need Brain-Based Wellness?

A recent report suggested that for the majority of North Americans over the age of 50, the number one fear is not whether they will have enough money to see them comfortably through their retirement; it's not even whether they will live a long and healthy life. The number one fear for people age 50 and over is losing their mental capacity.

Sadly, cerebral decline for many is becoming a greater possibility, with instances of Alzheimer's and dementia continuing to rise. In fact, just last month there was a major report suggesting that by the end of 2015 the number of people diagnosed with Alzheimer's will rise by 400 percent.

The rise in cases of Alzheimer's and dementia have a direct correlation to our society's rising and continual stress levels and the high levels of adrenaline and epinephrine that this causes in our brains. Continuous and excessive exposure to these stress hormones can interfere with our normal neurotransmitter activity. Neurotransmitters are endogenous chemicals that transmit signals from a neuron to a target cell across a synapse. They are responsible for making us feel good, but when they are not working properly, as is the case with people who are continually stressed, we end up feeling down, which can lead to depression. This is why people can often suffer from depression for no outward reason. This type of depression is caused by a lack of serotonin and other chemicals in the brain that keep us balanced.

Sympathetic Survival Syndrome

Cortisol is considered the most powerful hormone in the human body. This is because cortisol's job is survival, thus it can override the signals of every other hormone. When daily doses of cortisol become excessive, Sympathetic Survival Syndrome develops and the effects can be dangerous and debilitating, ranging from anxiety and depression to heart disease, dementia and cancer.

Cortisol is referred to as a master hormone. One of its functions is to tell the body to stop tapping into fat, which our brain needs to function. Our brain is, in fact, 70 percent fat; it uses the fat stores from our body to turn into energy. If there are high levels of cortisol in the brain, it functions as a barrier, stopping the brain from tapping into the body's fat reserves. This means that the brain has to cannibalize itself in order to function. This cannibalization leads to shrinking of the brain, which causes some of the diseases we have already discussed, such as Alzheimer's.

One side-effect of pervasive stress is adrenal exhaustion, which is in direct correlation to the constant production and over-production of epinephrine (adrenaline) in the brain. Adrenal exhaustion can have very serious consequences, one of which is sleep disturbance. Whether you have trouble falling asleep or trouble staying asleep, insomnia is another epidemic that is sweeping through our population, affecting around 40 million people in the US alone. Sleep disorders in themselves can be distressing to the individual suffering, but there are many more dangerous side effects including low blood sugar, constant fatigue, low immune function, anxiety, and depression which lead in turn to the abuse of alcohol, food or drugs to cope with the symptoms.

Looking at this list as a doctor, you should be able to pinpoint which of your patients are displaying these classic signs and symptoms of Sympathetic Survival Syndrome, those who are suffering from adrenal exhaustion and whose cortisol levels are at an all-time high. Sadly, though, the tragic effects of stress don't end there.

Other Devastating Effects of Stress

Chronic stress can lead to high blood pressure and undue strain on the heart. Our body's natural response to stress is to trigger a rapid release of glucose and fatty acids into the bloodstream. This is how your body can respond with strength and stamina during an emergency. However, the added glucose, if unused by the body, can cause elevated or erratic blood sugar levels. These blood sugar swings can make you feel fatigued and can lead to diabetes. The stress-related release of cortisol can also cause a build up of cholesterol in the arteries.

During periods of high stress, cortisol and epinephrine course through the body and signal non-essential functions to stop or slow down so that all systems essential to dealing with an emergency receive an extra boost. The immune system, which is not essential for urgent activity, temporarily stops or slows down during these peak stress periods. This system works out fine when the stress is short term, but when the stress hormones are continually pouring into the body, the immune system suffers, making you vulnerable to infection or deadly diseases such as cancer.

Osteoporosis is a big concern for most women once they reach a certain age. Of course we've all heard that you need to have plenty of calcium in your diet to help prevent osteoporosis, but most people probably don't realize that the best way to guard against osteoporosis is to keep the body in harmony. Keeping blood pressure regulated helps balance the levels of cortisol in the body, meaning that you're not eating up your bone density.

Another of the physical problems caused by high levels of stress is muscle wasting. A lot of the patients that we see do not exercise enough, or in some cases not at all. They don't understand that you need muscle to help regulate your metabolism. So it's not just causing mental health problems but physical ones as well.

Most of the people reading this will be carrying a little extra weight around the middle, nothing too harmful you might think, but you'd be wrong. Having that extra weight around the middle is a pretty good sign that you have insulin resistance, meaning that your cortisol levels are increasing slowly overtime.

Brain Waves Tell All

There are four primary brain wave frequencies, but today most people spend nearly all of their time in just one—beta mode. This is the frequency in play when we are reactionary; thus, it's called the reactionary mind. Beta mode is a normal state of alertness. We need it to be able to drive a car or read an instruction manual. In fact, we need it to do all sorts of things that require conscious attention. However, it is also the only brain wave frequency that allows for fear, anger, frustration or negative thinking. The problems start when the brain gets out of balance. When we have high levels of beta waves, it represses the normal functions of the other waves in our brain that allow us to wind down, relax and be joyful and creative.

A lot of people today are unable to get into a proper deep sleep because a natural cycle of sleep can't happen when we go to bed in beta mode. When we first start to fall asleep, we switch to predominantly alpha mode; we call this the intuitive mind. Once in alpha mode, we are in a state of relaxation or light meditation. Alpha mode is also associated with quiet times in our lives such as when we are involved in creative pursuits or prayer. Now if you've trained your brain then you can know that you've used your hour of power, you've done everything you can to; this is why prayers have been so important in the past, they allow you to focus your mind and attention. Now if you are a young child—at an age before you learned to be stressed—or if you've trained your brain properly, then the alpha waves can properly flow into theta waves.

Theta mode is the inventive part of your mind, which is why we call it the inventive mind. It's the activity of the brain that can help you to solve the problems in your life. You may heard the stories of great inventors who intentionally go to sleep with a problem posed on their minds, so that they end awakening with a solution. They get a brief peek into what we refer to as the super-conscious part of their mind.

Proper brain wave activity is essential to good health, both mentally and physically. The brain needs to go through these different brain wave states every day, and it especially needs time to allow the alpha and theta states to work properly.

The problem is, most people are spending little or no time in their intuitive and inventive minds—alpha and theta modes. They have trained themselves to deal with stress with their reactionary mind alone—beta mode. In other words, they are reacting to life instead of living it.

Moreover, when we're not sleeping properly, our brains don't spend enough time in the alpha and theta modes and, therefore, cannot recharge properly. Those who snore may be interested to know that snoring prevents the brain from going through these proper sleep cycles. Instead of going through beta, alpha and theta stages to get to delta (deep sleep) it tries to skip from beta straight to delta, skipping right past the alpha and theta stages.

Think of the alpha and theta stages of sleep as time for doing paperwork in the brain. It's when the brain stores, categorizes and organizes the day's activities so that the things that are meaningful and useful are systematically encoded and organized in a way that your subconscious can access them for future use. Trying to do everything in beta mode is almost like saying, "I want to have a great business, but I don't want to do all the paperwork that comes with it." Anyone with common sense knows that simply won't work.

We simply can't learn or remember well in beta mode. We need alpha and theta modes to properly process all of the information that we've gathered throughout the day. This is why people under extreme stress develop poor memories and muddled thinking.

The main thing to remember is that beta mode, the wide-awake, alert state, is also the reactionary mind where stress, fear and negative thinking happen. Delta is deep sleep, a state we all need to reach so the body can rebuild, repair and renew, and otherwise access the innate intelligence that keeps our bodies functioning. But we also need those times between awake and asleep, the alpha and theta modes. Whether it's through mindful meditation, relaxation techniques, yoga, painting, or fishing by stream, to live a balanced, happy life, you need those periods when your brain gets the chance to tap into these essential mid-point brain waves.

Meditation is a really important technique to help us to get out of beta and into alpha and theta modes. Many people find it extremely helpful in calming their minds and dealing with the stresses of life. Later in this chapter, we're going to introduce you to an alternative to meditation, a way to rapidly and dramatically get the results of meditation in a much more powerful state, and a lot quicker than using meditation. There is truly some amazing technology out there that can help us overcome the effects of our overloaded lifestyles.

Now that we've accurately and thoroughly discussed the problem of stress, the different forms of stress and how people are being trapped in Sympathetic Survival Mode. And now that we understand how cortisol and epinephrine levels affect the brain and how it can burn out our adrenals, let's turn our attention to solutions.

To assist yourself, your family and your patients in dealing with stress there are only a few things that we know for certain will help the brain get back into harmony, reboot and re-energize. Regular chiropractic adjustments, meditation, deep breathing, exercise and getting proper nutrition will all help. There are other methods of course, but these are the most well known and the most practiced.

If we look at some of the pioneers of the chiropractic profession such as George Goodheart, we can see how these innovators intuitively knew the relationship between pain and the brain. Going back some 50 years, after George Goodheart adjusted a patient, he would have them go for a walk, because intuitively he discovered that for those who walked after an adjustment, the brain would go back to a more balanced state a lot quicker, and it was this observation that led to his founding of Applied Kinesiology.

What you have learned so far is important, but the application of this information—what you'll learn in the following chapters—is even more important. Helping your patients to put this knowledge to good use will make all the difference in getting great results, establishing a wonderful reputation and becoming highly profitable; and of course this applies to both you and your practice.

"No matter how closely you examine the water, glucose, and electrolyte salts in the human brain, you can't find the point where these molecules became conscious."

-Deepak Chopra

CHAPTER

TWO

What is Brain-Based Wellness?

What is Brain-Based Wellness?

What is Brain-Based Wellness and why is it important? This is the fundamental question that will underpin this book. It will serve to provide you, the chiropractic doctor, with the core information surrounding Brain-Based Wellness, and help you recognize what you already know, what you need to know, and how to implement it in your practice. It will provide you with everything you need to know to move your practice into a new position of authority and success.

Now you may find yourself asking what has Brain-Based Wellness got to do with me? How is it going to help me in my practice? Of course, the fundamental core of any successful chiropractic practice is to adjust the patient, remove interference between the creator and the creation and let the power that made the body heal the body. However, increasingly, we are realizing that there is more to healing a patient then merely dealing with the physical. When the brain and body are in balance, great things can and usually do happen.

A patient can walk out of the office having had their adjustment done, but they're still going to be carrying all the stresses of life, which today are even greater than ever. A more comprehensive discussion of this can be found in Thrive in Overdrive, How to Navigate Your Overloaded Lifestyle by Dr. Porter.

Today's technology was created with a view to making our lives easier. Unfortunately, the reverse is true; it is actually making life increasingly more difficult and far more stressful.

Stress is the most pervasive malady of our time; indeed it has been labeled as the "silent killer." Often people don't recognize the symptoms of stress and just how harmful it can be until it is too late. We are 'plugged in' to the world 24/7 with our cell phones and the Internet; there is often no escape from the modern world and every day stress. In fact 90 percent of all illness and disease is stress related according to The National Institutes of Health.

There is a key message to today's chiropractor in this: When we're treating the body alone, we are only dealing with the symptoms of the illness, not the underlying cause.

In fact, when we're feeling good psychologically and we're not under all of the stresses and strains of modern life, the brain releases neuro-chemicals that make us feel good. These neuro-chemicals have a natural analgesic effect that can actually mask physical pain.

However, the opposite is also true. When we're under stress, different neuro-chemistry is released along with cortisol and epinephrine. This mix will usually go right to the weakest points of the body and create pain in those areas. Sadly, most people won't seek help from a doctor until the pain shows up, not realizing that the pain, caused by the hormones and neuro-chemicals emitted due to the stress response, could have been prevented.

Just take a moment to think about your typical patient. If I were to ask you what percentage of your patients you believe are truly stressed, what would you say? Most practitioners when asked this question would respond with a figure of around 90 percent—if not 100 percent. Almost all of us have stress of some kind—stress over work or home, money or time.

Today we consider driving a car an ordinary daily task. However, to your body, there is nothing ordinary about moving 70 miles an hour down a freeway with other cars and trucks barreling along the road beside you.

A study released at the 2013 annual meeting of the American Society of Hypertension in San Francisco found that talking on a mobile phone causes systolic blood pressure – the higher number in a blood pressure reading and the number doctors pay more attention to as a risk factor for cardiovascular disease – to rise significantly. Additionally, mobile phone use has been shown to consistently spike beta brain wave activity, adding significant stress to an already overtaxed brain.

Yoga is currently a $6 billion business and ranks as one of

the fastest growing industries. Relaxation drinks are a \$521 million industry and growing, and luxury massage chairs are a \$250 million industry. They are all focused on the business of relieving stress.

While there are three types of stress in life—physical, chemical and emotional—most experts agree that emotional stress is by far the most detrimental.

This is why we have written this book. We want to give doctors of chiropractic the tools, knowledge, and skills of a mind-based and brain-based wellness program to enable them to maximize their clinical results, grow their reputation and be rewarded accordingly.

The Neurological Epidemic

The most dangerous and hidden epidemic of the 21st Century is without a doubt the Neurological Epidemic which manifests itself more and more in disorders such as Alzheimer's, Parkinson's, Epilepsy, Autism, Migraines and Insomnia, to name but a few. As we've already discussed, this Neurological Epidemic is a result of the fast-paced, high-tech, high-stress lifestyle that everyone is leading in this new era of almost complete connectivity and never-ending stress.

When we're under stress our bodies are pumping out adrenaline and cortisol and trapping us in what we earlier referred to as Sympathetic Survival Syndrome, which is a defense physiology. This is an important term that we're introducing here, so we will take a moment to explain more thoroughly what we mean when we discuss Sympathetic Survival Syndrome.

When we're trapped in a sympathetic mode, we're stuck in fight-or-flight response, which is our innate mechanism designed to protect us from injury or attack. The problem with this response is that we're stuck on high alert; there is no room for exploration, consciousness or contribution. All of our abilities are focused on our survival instincts. If your patients are stuck in Sympathetic Survival Syndrome, it's very hard to get great clinical results with them. If you, as the practitioner, are stuck in Sympathetic Survival Syndrome, then it's a lot harder for you to grow your practice. How can you successfully grow a business— or be an innovative, loving, and kind person—when you're just trying to make ends meet?

The reality is that we cannot escape the fast-paced, high-tech, high-stress lifestyle of the 21st Century, so we have to learn new mechanisms to deal with the stresses of life to prevent it from causing problems for us, both physically and psychologically.

If you're reading this book, you no doubt already have some awareness of the benefits that a Brain-Based Wellness approach could have for your patients and your practice. When we first opened our practice 35 years ago, diseases such as Alzheimer's, Autism, and Chronic Fatigue were almost unheard of; they were rare diseases. Today serious neurological conditions such as these, where the brain is out of balance, are reaching almost epidemic proportions.

However, you may not be aware of just how big the benefits to you and your practice can be. There is a huge window of opportunity for us as practitioners to repositions ourselves as neurological experts— functional neurologists if you will. This can lead to us building an amazing reputation, attracting a large number of new patients, and significantly improving our compliance and retention; ultimately leading to substantial profitability.

What is brain stress?

Since 1988, the rate of anti-depressant use in the United States has increased 400 percent. 40 million American adults are affected with an anxiety disorder of some kind. 1 in 10 Americans aged 12 and over are currently taking anti-depressant medication, with drug use being most common between the 18 to 44 age brackets.

This is just a small selection of shocking statistics. We could probably fill half this book with more statistics of the same kind. What this undoubtedly shows is that all forms of stress lead to brain stress and it is this that is leading to the all-too-common occurrence of neurological problems and creating this window of opportunity for the chiropractic profession.

It's important for you to realize that every patient walking into your practice has an inner pharmacy. In fact, we all possess the most powerful pharmacy on Earth. It's the human brain, an incredible organ capable of releasing 30-thousand different neurochemicals with a simple thought.

So the aim and purpose of this book is to teach you how to train your patients to think the right thoughts that trigger the release of healthy neurochemistry, the kind that leads to a happy, fulfilling life. Today, for patients to truly achieve wellness, we must teach them to manage their stress and learn how to cope with an ever-changing environment, because in today's world, we simply can't eliminate stress completely. We need to teach our patients (and ourselves) effective coping mechanisms to protect us from the psychological effects of stress and to help our brains keep up with the fast-paced world that we live in so our brains can do the jobs they were designed to do.

Why is Brain Stress so dangerous?

Well, here's another statistic for you. More than 2 billion people worldwide currently suffer from brain-based health challenges. All forms of stress, whether it is stress about a relationship, time, job, money, or emotional stress, all in reality are a form of brain stress. This is another important term that we want to introduce to you.

You may not be fully aware of brain stress, but you and your patients are all suffering from it in one form or another and we're going to offer you some solutions.

Periods of defense physiology (fight-or-flight) need to be

followed by a recovery time. Today people are consistently going back into stressful situations and not giving themselves the ability to recover. Over time, the brain habituates to the stress state and that's when we become trapped in beta mode, setting the stage for poor quality of life, physical decline and for disease to take hold.

Whenever defense physiology kicks in, the body goes into high alert with all of the reactions and responses that go with it. Heart rate, blood pressure, sugar levels and respiration rates all increase while gastro-intestinal and immune activity decrease and pupils dilate. All of this is useful and perfectly normal when we're faced with a stressor of any kind and the body is preparing for fight-or-flight, the problem comes when we don't allow our bodies down time from this kind of stress, therefore limiting our ability to recover.

Some of the latest and hottest business books out there tell us that the most productive people in business have these power hours of high performance ranging from ninety minutes to three hours. Within these windows there is complete focus on the problem or project on hand. It's high intensity, high concentration and productivity followed by a recovery period. You can have two or three of these high intensity windows in a typical day, but they have to be followed by an hour or two of recovery time so the brain can do its processing and then re-engage.

This is also fully consistent with what we know about the exercise world. The hottest trend in exercise, based on all of the current research, is high intensity interval training, working really hard for short periods of time and then having a recovery period.

So the underlying problem and the reason why Sympathetic Survival Syndrome—defense physiology—is such a problem in today's society is that people are not recovering; they are not taking the time out after a high intensity period to allow their bodies and minds to recoup. Too much of the fight-or-flight response without the corresponding rest and relaxation is what distress is all about.

Your sympathetic nervous system is about survival and your parasympathetic nervous system is about healing and recovery. Your sympathetic system is involved in fight-or-flight and your parasympathetic system about rest-and-digest.

During fight-or-flight response, our adrenal glands go into overdrive. Most chiropractic practitioners are seeing more and more patients suffering from stressed—if not completely shut down—adrenals. These patients simply can't handle the continual drive to the extreme. As we have already noted, this is a huge problem in today's society, this continual turned on fight-or-flight response manifests itself in disease and behavioral problems to the epidemic proportions that we're seeing today.

As chiropractors we have the ability to take the stressful edge off and rebalance the nervous system. There are tools at our disposal that can easily and effectively allow us to bring the nervous system back into harmony, away from its fight-or-flight state into one of calm and relaxation to allow the body to heal and recover properly.

The true purpose of the chiropractic adjustment is to normalize and maximize brain function.

With the constant state of stress showing up in our lives and our patients' lives, we will need to regularly reboot, rebalance, reset and restore balance and harmony between the sympathetic-parasympathetic systems within our brains and nervous systems.

Here is the simple but profound summary...

All forms of stress cause brain stress. When the brain is stressed, it goes out of balance and unfortunately, the body always follows and goes out of balance as well. This shows up as illness, disease, behavioral problems, loss of vitality and rapid aging. The chiropractic adjustment rebalances the brain and when the brain is balanced again, fortunately, the body will follow and heal.

CHAPTER

THREE

What is Self-Mastery Technology?

What is Self-Mastery Technology?

This section will begin to address some of the self-mastery techniques out there that might be able to help people correct brain stress better, faster and more permanently. Most people are aware that they should be doing something, that they need to be doing something; the problem is that they have no idea what that something is. They either don't have the tools or they set the bar too high, they have expectations that are unachievable.

Stress is unfortunately part of life, and in the 21st Century it has become a more prevalent problem than ever before in human history. What people have to realize is that they're not going to find a magic solution to get rid of stress completely; instead they should be focusing on finding a way to control the stress and find ways to cope with it better. We have to start accepting that we're never going to be completely stress free, but we can neutralize it and allow ourselves to rebalance and heal more effectively.

The number one thing about Self-Mastery Technology is that we have to change our belief systems. We have to have the faith that we can feel great. We simply don't have to feel lousy and stressed all the time.

Not only do you deserve to be happy, so do your patients. This cannot be achieved by inaction, there has to be some action on your part and on the part of the patient, but you also have to be aware that it's not going to happen overnight.

The important thing is to take action every day, no matter how small; take one action every day that will work towards your bigger, long-term goals. It's not just doing it once and then you're fixed. This is something that has to be worked at over time. In fact, someone once asked me if Self-Mastery Technology was addictive? My response was, "I don't know, I've been doing it since I was 12 years old!"

My Dad was very much into using self-help strategies; he taught us about affirmations and how to visualize and meditate on the results you want to achieve. We used these techniques for sports, but they can apply to any and every part of your life. The great thing about the brain is that once you start to use these techniques in one part of the brain, it generalizes into other areas of your life. If we can focus our minds on the solutions to the smaller, everyday problems that we face, our brains will start to hardwire themselves to be able to deal with the larger problems in the same way.

An Overview of Self-Mastery Technology?

Some of you reading this may already be familiar with Self-Mastery Technology (SMT), but for those who aren't, I am going to give a brief overview. The foundation of SMT is the MindFit Neuro-Trainer™. When patients undergo SMT, they simply lie back with their eyes closed and the MindFit's precise frequencies of light and sound waves are fed into the brain using specially designed headphones and glasses. The light pulses are picked up by the optic nerve and even though the patient cannot consciously discern any difference, there is actually a slight frequency difference between the two. It works like binaural beats, or beats just using sound, which only 10 percent of the population can discern and respond to.

Light and sound is used in SMT because this is the structure of the brain. The brain uses light and sound to create our space and place in the universe. When we walk into a room, our brain evaluates the light and sound and projects an image of the room. So the idea is that SMT helps us to balance the two hemispheres of the brain using the light and sound waves being projected. When the brain begins to synchronize, the body begins to synchronize. The brain is taken from beta mode and is guided with a very specific algorithm.

Now you might ask, How does the brain know to do that? This is where Dr. Alexander Kaplan's algorithms come into play. We've been studying how the brain responds to light and sound stimulus and what algorithms are needed since the early 80s. In fact, work continues on this today at Moscow State University where Dr. Kaplan, the developer of the SMT algorithms we use, is the head of the Human Brain Research Group.

You can even experience this with sounds, where the harmonics can be in the background guiding you from a normal state into a state of relaxation. Once the brain is fully relaxed, it can start to do self- adjustments. Once the body knows what it's like to be in the adjusted state where our innate intelligence tells us that this is normal function, we can begin to re-educate and reprogram our physiology and neurology to keep it that way.

I have one doctor who uses SMT four to five times a week. He tells me that each time his experience is different, and this is completely normal because the brain is plastic—it is always changing.

When people listen to SMT, they often sense the light blinking at different intensities. Sometimes they will hear my voice in their right ear, sometimes the left and sometimes both. Sometimes they'll even hear me having two different conversations with them at once. All of this takes place with the sound and the harmonics in the background and it all works in harmony to stimulate your brain to go back into balance.

That same doctor told me that he wished he had found this amazing tool when he was a child and not a man in his 50s.

SMT is truly changing lives. I've known people who were afraid of flying, but after a few sessions of SMT, it was not a problem. People who were trying to lose weight and failing after having been on every diet imaginable, after starting SMT started to lose weight naturally and effortlessly. Even people with insomnia who had resorted to sleeping pills to help, after a few sessions of SMT were sleeping through the night without sleep aids, waking up feeling energized and refreshed. The list goes on and on.

SMT is such an amazingly powerful tool, and it has the added benefit of being completely natural. My goal is to get more and more chiropractors to recognize the benefits that it can have for them and their patients, and for them to start using it in the practices.

Why should you master SMT?

You may be reading this wondering how and why chiropractors are perfectly positioned to start employing SMT in their clinics. Well, the important thing to remember, and this is sometimes too often forgotten or not recognized, is that chiropractic is a neuro-musculoskeletal science. The important part here is neuro and it's something that must never be overlooked. There is a very well known saying, "Mind over matter," which accurately sums this up. The mind is in control; it is dominant over the matter. In this case, matter is our physical bodies.

In chiropractic, we have always talked about the concept of above-down and from inside-out. Healing, balancing and maximizing what is above, our brain allows this enormous self-correcting process to then take place from above-down and then we express it from inside-out. As a chiropractor, I am totally a fan of anything that normalizes and maximizes brain and nervous system function and is natural. SMT does that exceedingly well in conjunction with specific and appropriate chiropractic adjustments.

It is also important to note that the majority of subluxations are created emotionally. DD Palmer, the father of chiropractic, discussed the 3Ts of subluxation: thoughts, traumas and toxins, but according to most experts about 80 percent of all subluxations are emotional, meaning it is another brain-based issue that is not being handled by the majority of chiropractors who choose to focus on the physical primarily and the chemical secondarily. Again, every physical adjustment helps to normalize and maximize brain function.

This is a huge shift in our thinking. Until recently most chiropractors have been of the mindset that the adjustment works to just relieve nerve pressure. Of course it does, but this is not the only benefit as it also helps to normalize and maximize brain function. This is a crucial development that I hope everyone reading this book will take note of and start to utilize in their everyday practices.

It was only a few years ago that scientists were still reinforcing the idea that the brain was fixed, that the brain could not and does not change. Of course we now know that this is completely wrong, in fact the brain and the nervous system are extremely flexible, and always open to change for better or for worse. This incredible ability to change is called neuroplasticity.

Unfortunately this change is not always for the best. Oftentimes the stresses of our everyday lives can make it change for the worse. Through the system that we will outline in this book, we know for a fact that we can get your and your patient's brains to go back to a better, healthier, and younger, more vibrant and balanced state.

We need to shift our thinking away from just attending to the physical problems of our patients, to that of the mental or emotional as well. It's important to recognize that pain hurts, but stress kills.

Most people will come to a chiropractor, even a wellness chiropractor, because they are in pain; it is a natural progression that when you are in pain, you want to find a way to deal with that pain and to get rid of it. This is why we need to recognize that if we want to heal the body, we must heal the brain first. Once the brain is balanced, the body will always follow. Not the other way around.

Roger Sperry was a neuropsychologist and neurobiologist who won the Nobel Prize for physiology or medicine in 1981. He said that, "Ninety percent of the stimulation and nutrition to the brain is generated by the movement of the spine."

So Sperry was saying back in the 1980s what we're saying today; that it's the spine and the adjustments that we do to the spine that normalize and maximize the brain. This is just another of the many reasons why, in our opinion, chiropractors are perfectly poised to take control of and utilize this new field, Brain-Based Wellness, which is something that we will discuss and outline in more detail further along in this book.

In fact, we've been working on this approach since the 80s. Dr Stan Hugo, who has passed away now, was instrumental in allowing the concept of Brain-Based Wellness into his clinics. He was aware that when his patients were more relaxed and more at peace, his adjustments would work better; they would be more effective. He operated a Wholeness Clinic at the time, so called because he worked on the whole body. We found then in that environment that we could work well together, and as I still believe today that when somebody is stress-free, then everything works better. To put it another way: What the brain thinks, the body follows.

The Wellness Revolution

More and more people are seeing chiropractors not as a means to get well but as a means to stay well. This wellness revolution is being led by the Baby Boomers, the first generation in history that's unwilling to accept aging and decline as an inevitably. Rather, they are proactively seeking out ways to maintain vibrant health and an active lifestyle well into old age.

Most chiropractors are unaware of this shift and of their ever-changing role in society. However, their role has indeed changed from being a means to deal with a pain that is already there, to one of preventing the pain in the first place. People are becoming more and more aware of their bodies, and the fact that it's important to take care of the body to prevent problems arising in the first place; they are looking to chiropractors because they are concerned with wellness, not with sickness.

As an example, there are currently 35 million users of an online brain training program called Lumosity, with 100,000 new people signing up for the program every day. Lumosity is a neuroscience research company and they are experts in the field of enhancing brain performance through brain games.

The concept of Brain-Based Wellness continues to gain momentum, thanks to the work of people such as Dr. Richard Barwell, Daniel Amen, Mark Hyman, Rob Melillo, Joe Dispenza, Ted Carrick and Patrick Porter. All of these people have been leading the charge on Brain-Based Wellness for a long time, and now is the time to take control and reintegrate it into the chiropractic profession and every day practice.

It's ironic that in order to advance the profession of chiropractic we're actually going backwards to what chiropractic was based on in the first place, which was all about neurological function, and all of this comes back to Self-Mastery Technology.

SMT stimulates the brain with the right combination of light and sound to release the right chemicals to help balance the brain. These are the chemicals that are naturally released when we have a pleasurable experience, or when we're in a state of learning, so that our memory, concentration and creativity all improve.

Most of the algorithms that we're working with, especially within Dr. Porter's series, are those focusing on attention deficit disorders. The aim is to be able to teach you to help your patients bring out their alpha and beta intact so they will be able to interact with the world with a more relaxed mindset, getting the brain to work in harmony with the world.

Now the reality is that you could spend twenty years with Buddhist monks learning how to meditate and focus your mind, or in a seminary in the mountains, but the reality is that most of us can't do that.

In today's turned-on and tuned-in environment, the only way to ensure that the brain stays in its full spectrum mode is to train it to do so using full spectrum light and sound training. We need to ensure that all our brain waves are in balance, and it's important to remember that no one brain wave is superior to another; they all have a function in our lives and balance is essential.

SMT was originally developed to help people with chronic pain issues that were unable to use biofeedback as a means to relieve their pain. Being in pain has the side effect of being stuck in beta mode, because it's the only place where pain exists.

The great thing about SMT is it helps the brain balance beta, alpha and theta waves, thus allowing the body to create a pain-free state. It also helps to create the proper flow of the neurochemicals through the brain and the body, so that the body and mind are able to work together in harmony.

We've found that one of the side benefits of the brain and body being in balance is that innate intelligence is able to take over and wonderful things begin to happen. Incredible transitions begin to take place. The body naturally shifts into a healing state, enabling a more active lifestyle because the body is more relaxed.

What does the research have to say?

It's important to note that up to 100 percent of excess adrenaline is flushed from the system every time the body achieves the relaxation response—which is the opposite of the fight-or-flight response. This alone is a dramatic result considering that over-production and retention of adrenaline is one of the most dangerous side effects of stress because it adds to the toxic burden of the body.

One of the most important neurochemicals that is released during an SMT session is norepinephrine; in fact, research shows there is an 11 percent rise in the patient's levels of norepinephrine after just one session.

I know that some of you reading this already have SMT in your office. If you've ever had a patient say, "Hey, why do I feel so good?" after an SMT session, it's primarily due to the rise in norepinephrine levels.

Additionally, the same research showed that serotonin levels increase by 21 percent on average. This helps the brain eliminate excess stress chemicals, which is of course the desired outcome. The problem is that serotonin is designed to be brought into the brain, used and then flushed out; this is one of the major problems with traditional anti-depressant medications, which are designed to keep serotonin in the brain longer. It can be likened to keeping food in your refrigerator and thinking that if you keep it longer, it's going to taste better, it's not. In the same way, storing serotonin in the brain is not going to make it work better.

Dr. Roger K. Cady, Dr. Norman Shealy in "Neurochemical Responses to Cranial Electrical Stimulation and Photo-Stimulation via Brain Wave Synchronization. "Study performed by the Shealy Institute of Comprehensive Health Care, Springfield, Missouri, 1990, 11 pp.: Eleven patients had peridural and blood analysis performed before and after the relaxation sessions using flash emitting goggles. An average increase of beta-endorphin levels of 25% and serotonin levels of 21% were registered. The beta-endorphin levels are comparative to those obtained by cranial electrical stimulation (CES). This indicates a potential decrease of depression related symptoms when using photic stimulation.

Used serotonin needs to be flushed out to allow the brain to create new neuro-chemicals and restore balance. The brain knows how to create these balanced pain-free states; it's just that the chemical reactions occur in the body based on the brain wave state we're in. When we're trapped in high beta mode, we don't have the alpha and theta patterns to tell the brain to create new neurochemicals, because it's stuck in fight-or-flight mode. So we need to ensure that the sympathetic system is able to relax and interact with life instead of always reacting to it.

Another one of the great things about SMT versus other methods of dealing with stress is that there are no side effects to the technology. We tell people in our clinic that the only side effect is that you may fall asleep and have a good nap, and you can wake up and your life will change for the better. There really are no negative side effects to using this technology.

The only contraindication would be patients who have epilepsy or other seizure disorders. For these people we don't use the light portion of the device. Fortunately, these people can still get exceptional results with SMT because the light frequency is only one of four technologies that are involved in the SMT algorithms.

So whether your aim is to improve your learning, balance brain waves, normalize blood pressure, improve your energy, lift your mood, eliminate addiction or become more assertive, you will find that all of these are side-benefits, rather than side effects, of using SMT. When the brain is in balance, everything else will follow.

So we know through neurological research that when the neurons start firing together they also start wiring together. This means that we're actually teaching the brain to wire itself to achieve new levels of efficiency, and the brain loves it. The brain is like a muscle. It is designed to be used.

Conversely, if the brain is sedentary, such as passively watching TV all the time, it begins to lose the new levels of wiring that you have worked so hard to create. This is why Lumosity is so popular. The brain wants to be functioning and used, and a brain game is one way to do it. SMT is another way, a fun way that lets you relax back and take a "nap" while your brain is getting its neurological exercise.

We've had dozens of open and real-time live sessions with skilled NeuroInfiniti™ doctors (neurologically-based chiropractors) in which we are able to track the brain waves from the patient's wide-awake state into the relaxation response. Like clockwork, we see the beta brain waves come down as alpha and theta go up, until balance is achieved.

We'd just briefly like to share with you an experience that we had at NeuroInfiniti™ training with Dr. Richard Barwell and his team. Dr. Barwell hooked up one of the doctors and we could watch on the TV screen how this doctor's brain was out of balance. We started off seeing how his sympathetic and parasympathetic systems were firing at completely different rates. They hooked him up to a Self-Mastery Technology session and after six or seven minutes you could see on the screen how the brain started to come back into balance and harmony; the sympathetic and parasympathetic systems were soon firing equally. It was a jaw dropping experience for most people in that room, to visually see the brain come back into balance.

There is also a lot of research that suggests that simply taking a mid-day nap can be very beneficial. We jokingly say that an SMT session is like taking a nap on steroids. It helps to stimulate the process of flushing out the excess cortisol and adrenaline from the system and bringing the system back into balance, in much the same way that you do every night when you enter a deep sleep.

SMT in the chiropractic practice

We have over 600 alternative health clinics now using this technology and many of our practitioners tell us that they use it in the middle of the afternoon so that when their evening patients come in, they are recharged and ready to do their best work, even though it's the end of the day.

Statistically speaking, twenty minutes using Self-Mastery Technology is equivalent to about three to four hours of good sound sleep depending on how deep you go during those twenty minutes. It's almost the same equivalence with meditation: Twenty minutes of SMT can be equivalent to three to four hours of solid meditation. However, in reality you would probably require years of training in disciplined meditation to have the same effect as twenty minutes of SMT.

Most people, during meditation, don't get deep into theta or alpha. They might achieve five minutes at this state, but for the average person, this is about it. The problem most people have is they have some kind of attention deficit, meaning that their attention wanders. The minute the mind starts to wander, you are no longer meditating and no longer in the deep theta or beta states. The great thing about SMT-style neuro-training is that we can actually track the brain patterns during and after its use.

We sometimes refer to SMT technology as PX90 for the brain. People tend to know how to create an exercise program for their bodies and understand the importance of doing so, but they are at a complete loss when it comes to exercising the control center—their human brain.

For those of you unfamiliar with PX90, the program includes twelve intense workouts that use resistance and body-weight training, cardio, plyometrics, ab work, martial arts and yoga, along with a nutrition plan, fitness guide and workout calendar. The developers of this system recognized that they could achieve superior physical results by combining the best of what's out there.

With SMT, we took that same philosophy and applied it to brain wave entrainment. We combine neurosensory algorithms with psychoacoustics that trigger different parts of the brain and combine it with strategic mind-messaging, integrating language patterns, affirmations, and visualization exercises to stimulate positive, goal-oriented thinking. All of these individual pieces fit together to create a harmonic symphony for the brain.

We've tried to teach people meditation for around 25 years and this is what we hear: "I can't meditate… I can't sit still… I can't control my mind… I've got a million thoughts going round in my head at once."

These are all clues that you've got a brain wave imbalance problem and you need to bring your mind and body back into balance.

It's important for us to make sure that people are aware that this is not just something that we're making up; we've been doing research on the brain for many years. In the last two decades we've seen vast improvements in computer technologies and graphing programs that are able to track the brain waves of people experiencing SMT. With advancements in technology we have been able to go from a unit the size of a microwave to a unit smaller than a deck of cards. This has meant that the technology is now a lot more commercially viable and accessible to a larger number of people. Technology is continually shifting and the end results just continue to improve as we enhance the technology.

Through the other chapters in this book we're going to be showing you how to utilize this technology yourself and with your patients as you incorporate and implement it into your practice. We're going to be showing you everything you need to create a viable business model and marketing model and how this technology can go hand-in-hand with traditional ongoing chiropractic care.

In our opinion, this is the most effective back-end system from a profitability point of view we've ever found in chiropractic and we want you to feel the same way by the end of this book.

Throughout this book you will be learning all of this and more, even if you want to go solo and just use the information you learn here to educate your patients, you will have a new sense of confidence and a new identity; it will help you tremendously. Let's go further and actually talk about some MindFit with SMT programs.

This program is designed to help you and your patients overcome almost any problem or achieve just about any goal.

We've developed over 32 different series. Each one is designed to imprint positive suggestions into the mind of the user and integrate them so that they become habits. There's a saying that we like to use with our patients: You get what you rehearse in life, not necessarily what you intend."

We often tell people that conscious commitment leads to subconscious action. By learning this visualization process, it allows you to rehearse the things that you want and desire so that the subconscious can no longer tell the difference between real or imagined, so that you can begin to implement them into your life immediately, one day at a time. The patient actually begins to think, act or respond as though the changes are already locked into their subconscious.

Summary

Let's just take a few minutes to go over some of the key points from this module for you to remember and utilize. First, you get what you rehearse in life, not necessarily what you intend. Managing your stress is the best first step to achieving vitality, health and wellness, both mentally and physically for yourself, your family, your staff and your patients.

At the end of every module we're going to give you a task to complete to help you on your journey, we'll outline this more at the end of this chapter but for the moment we'll just say that you should take time every day to use the technology yourself, starting with TMC1: Experience the Tools of Mastery.

With TMC 1 you're going to get all components of SMT except the lights, unless you already have a MindFit Neuro-Trainer. So what will happen is that you're going to use the earphones because they're going to be programmed with the sensory algorithms. You want to find a quiet place where you can use it at least once a day, where you can kick back, close your eyes and relax; some people even use it twice a day.

Doing this is going to help to train the brain to get the different brain frequencies, there are going to be minor beats and the sensory algorithms; the music that is encoded to work with them and what we call the psychoacoustics. So even if you don't have the lights yet, listen with the earphones, take a little nap, and enjoy it. Make sure you position yourself somewhere that you won't be disturbed for 20 minutes so that you can be integrating all you're learning through the tools of mastery and reading this book. Practicing this every day you're going to see your reputation take off and your income will follow.

We've only just begun to scratch the surface of the benefits that following and implementing this program is going to have on you and your practice. Over the next few chapters we're going to be adding to your vocabulary and experiences and help you to really build from the inside-out; we want you to make this part of your everyday life. This new focus will give you a new and improved way to communicate what you do as a chiropractor and it will change the conversation in your practice away from treating symptoms and toward achieving high level, well...Brain Based Wellness.

Once it becomes part of your personal experience and you're less stressed people are going to notice, they're going to say, Wow, what's going on doc?" and you're going to be able to tell them about the mind and brain-based part of your program.

Assignment

Your assignment for this module is to do some research. We want you to take some time to evaluate your stressors and consider the health changes that will help keep your cortisol levels low.

We also want you to consider your staff, how you can help keep their cortisol levels low, and then think about your patients and how you can help them. We want to change the conversation in practice, we want you to make a list of your stressed patients; who are they? Even if 100% of your patients make the list we want you to refer to them from now on as your stressed patients so that we can find a formula for helping them.

But of course before you can help other people, you have to help yourself. Create an action plan for your own personal brain health. What's your first step? What would be your second step? Your third, fourth and fifth? Once you've created your own action plan you can create a similar one for everyone in your practice.

C H A P T E R

F O U R

How to Add $50,000 or More to Your Bottom Line

How to add $50 thousand or more to your bottom line

Before we delve into this chapter and the numerous ways in which you can add income to your bottom line, we just want to clarify that the focus always has been, and always will be, on the patient. This system was designed to help your patients who have a brain imbalance or brain stress. If they're the type of patient that we've already discussed in earlier chapters we want to help them achieve brain balance to be healthier and more adaptive.

The added benefit is that you can add $50 thousand, $100 thousand or more to your bottom line.

You will find that if you focus on finding the solution for your patients and making their lives better, then the money that you want to make from your business will follow. As we said in previous chapters, high-stress levels, poor health and sleep disorders are reaching epidemic proportion. If you can provide an effectual, cost effective and natural solution to your patients, they're going to keep coming back, and they're going to refer their friends. Your practice will grow naturally through great patient care and you can start adding to your bottom line. Truly a win for all.

Again, I know we've said it a few times now, but it's worth repeating, because it really is the most important part of this whole program, the patient and their interests must take priority, the side effect is the profitability that comes your way.

Our most important rule is this: Whatever we recommend to the patient must always be in the patient's best interest and must best serve the individual; and then it should also be profitable to you the doctor.

The emergence of Sympathetic Survival Syndrome and Brain-Based Wellness is of extreme importance. Stress, and the diseases that it causes, is reaching epidemic proportions in our modern society and it's only getting worse. If you were to take an honest evaluation of your patients, the overwhelming majority of them are stressed and suffering from diseases associated with it. They come into the office and they report that they are stressed at work and at home. They are culturally stressed. Sometimes it's time stress, activity stress or relationship stress.

Chiropractic patients most certainly have health stress or they wouldn't be in your office in the first place. Whatever it is that is placing them under so much stress, it will inevitably lead to brain stress, and its brain stress that throws the brain out of balance and when the brain goes out of balance, inevitably the body will go out of balance as well.

We've already been through a whole host of physiological-neurological-chemical reactions that result from brain stress in the previous chapters. These reactions put people into Sympathetic Survival Syndrome; the sympathetics are continually revved up with little or no time for recovery, which leads to tremendous problems for the patient on every level. We also discussed in the previous chapters how this creates an amazing window of opportunity for you to really grow a practice, rebrand yourself, dramatically increase your referrals, improve your retention, clinical results and ultimately improve your bottom-line.

Let's take a few moments to go back and briefly review Sympathetic Survival Syndrome. All forms of stress cause sympathetic and parasympathetic imbalance. When the stress is ongoing, it creates a neurological cascade of events that leads to Sympathetic Survival Syndrome.

When we're stuck in survival mode our ability to heal, grow, love and flourish is greatly diminished. The brain and nervous system are both greatly compromised. Today the number of people who are trapped in sympathetic survival syndrome is reaching epidemic proportions. People are constantly in fight-or-flight mode, with little or no time for recovery. It's our job to help our patients to learn how to unwind, rebalance and heal themselves from above-down and then from inside-out.

Why is stress such a problem today?

Now you may be wondering, what's so different about stress today compared to 50, 20 or even ten years ago? Stress is obviously something that has had a constant presence throughout the ages. The stress response has been evolving over thousands of years, originally as a survival technique.

So why is it now that brain stress is reaching epidemic proportions? Well, as we've already suggested, the problems associated with stress are becoming so prevalent in today's society because we're constantly bombarded with stimulus from cell phones and electronics. We are constantly exposed to electromagnetic frequencies, colorings and dyes and preservatives, noise pollution, and traffic. We have money worries, family and career worries, global uncertainties and a new pressure to multi-task. The list goes on and on.

Even modern entertainment has a negative stress-effect. Rather than sitting on a quiet river bank fishing or gathering around a fire with family and fellow tribe members to sing and chant as our ancestors did, we plant ourselves in front of 60 inch high-definition television screens watching shows depicting upsetting or terrifying situations, blinding violence and non-stop action. And, since apparently that's not enough, we also add booming surround-sound systems to make it all the more real. Because your brain doesn't know the difference between real and imagined, it reacts to these stressful portrayals as if it were real to you.

This really is a new generation problem. In the past we only saw these kinds of stress reactions in people who were exposed to extreme stress, such as those who were in combat zones. Today more and more people's day-to-day lives are bombarded by stress like someone in a combat zone. Daily they are barraged by too much information and high-stress experiences and expectancies, and this is where chiropractors are now coming into a unique situation. People want to find a wellness-solution, a drug-free solution and a doctor-supervised solution to their stress problems and doctors of chiropractic are extremely well placed to provide that solution.

Electro-Magnetic Frequencies

We've already talked a little about electro-magnetic frequencies (EMF) and how they affect the brain; we're going to get into this a little more a bit further in, but be aware that electro-magnetic frequencies are everywhere. Between cell phones, televisions, microwaves, blow dryers, computer screens, fluorescent lights and airplanes to name a few, we're being bombarded with different electro-magnetic frequencies all the time.

These waves are damaging our own natural brain waves and neurological patterns. They have a detrimental effect on our health and the most scary thing of all is that the ordinary person on the street is completely unaware that it's happening, because EMF can't been seen, tasted, felt or measured in our day to day lives.

It's extremely important that we make ourselves aware of the negative effect that EMF has on our brains and our bodies so that we can communicate about these issues with our patients and work together to find a solution.

Several people have conducted studies about the long-term effects of using cell phones and the detrimental consequences that it can have on your health, but the majority of these studies have been conducted with the view to investigating whether cell phone use causes or leads to cancer.

Little is known or thought about the other effects that cell phone use can have on our brains and our brain wave states. For example, taking a brain scan while a patient is using a cell phone shows that the radiation eminating from the cell phone penetrates into your brain and goes all the way through to the other ear.

What's perhaps more important for our patients to know is that the radiation does not dissipate as soon as you finish your cell phone call. It stays in your brain for prolonged periods of time. It was additionally found that after cell phone use the brain wave patterns are abnormal and they stay that way for a period of time. This means that beta waves are being spiked for prolonged periods, resulting in the alpha and theta waves being diminished, which are, as we've already discussed, important to allow the brain to heal.

Conditioned Responses

Another example of this is the study conducted by Ivan Pavlov with his dogs. In his experiment, Pavlov used a bell as a neutral stimulus. Whenever he gave food to his dogs, a stimulus that caused salivation, he also rang a bell. After repeating this procedure a number of times, he tried ringing the bell without presenting the food. Surprisingly, the bell on its own now caused an increase in the dogs' salivation.

So the dogs had learned an association between the bell and the food and a new behavior was learned. Because this response was learned (or conditioned), it is called a conditioned response. The neutral stimulus (the bell) has now become a conditioned stimulus. Our bodies act something like Pavlov's dogs; they become conditioned over time. For example, every time we use our cell phones, the abnormal brain wave patterns are triggered and soon start to form a pattern. Next thing you know, those altered brain waves are happening even when we're not using our cell phones. This alteration in our brain waves can lead to lack of concentration, memory loss, inability to learn and aggressive behavior.

Children's brains are not patterned yet so they're a lot more susceptible to the re-patterning, which usually occurs naturally through our life experiences, but that is being altered by the excessive use of cell phones and technology. This is why it is so important that we teach people how to retrain the brain back into its natural state.

Attention Deficit Hyperactivity Disorder

In today's society, everyone has heard of ADHD, in fact most of us will know at least one person who has been diagnosed with this condition. It's interesting to note that before 1975 there was no such thing as ADHD; well, there was no such diagnosis. We have to take this into account when examining the statistics for ADHD, just because the statistics were low or non-existent in the past does not mean that there was no such thing as ADHD. One statistic is that the rate of parent-reported ADHD in children between the ages of 14 to 17 years of age sits at 22 percent between 2003 and 2007. These numbers reflect an increase of 42% among older teens.

Part of this increase has to be attributed to the fact that today's society is so much more fast-paced. Children are learning to do things in short bursts instead of sitting down and learning from a book the way we did when we were at school. Today children can just as easily watch a movie or TV program and get everything they need to know without ever having to read a book.

In 2007, there were approximately 5.4 million children, which is nearly 10 percent of school-aged children, that had received a diagnosis of ADHD. Unfortunately, that figure has likely continued to increase. Of those diagnosed children, 2.7 million are currently taking medication for their condition, which, we think you will agree, is an alarming statistic.

Of course, as with any medications, drugs used to treat ADHD have a myriad of side effects. We have to recognize that of shootings that take place in schools, for example, kids on some kind of psychotropic drugs perpetrated 100 percent of these terrible events.

Clearly better health through better chemistry is a belief and paradigm that has failed, which has left people seeking better and more natural solutions to their problems. We believe that Brain-Based Wellness is that solution.

So we've already got a large part of the population that would definitely benefit from a mind/brain-based wellness program.
The solution to our society's stress problem

We need someone to step up and say, "We have a solution to

this problem." Now you may find yourself being a little skeptical of these claims, but we can assure you that we are not just saying we have the answer, we have statistics to prove that we have the answer.

We conducted our first study in Arizona in the 80s when we first came out with MC2, the very first portable light-sound machine. We put our device in 30 chiropractic offices. All of the participants in the study were of school age and sitting on an average grade of B or lower; we found that within 3 months of using the light-sound technology, their average grades had gone up by at least 1 grade point, which meant that if you were a B student, you became an A student. This is why we designed the 3-month modules that we're going to discuss in later chapters, because just three months can make a huge difference.

We're not the only ones to have conducted studies in this area, Stanford University holds a symposium every year about brain-based wellness, although they call it brain-wave entertainment, but we're taking about the same thing. They also recognize the importance of the problem and that we need to tackle this as a community; the difference is that they're tackling it from a medical standpoint. They're investigating primarily how we can get people's brain waves back into balance and there are some phenomenal results coming out of the research that they're conducting. For example, Stanford hosted a symposium engaging experts in an interdisciplinary dialogue on the hypothesis that brain waves entrain to rhythmic auditory stimuli, a phenomenon known as auditory driving.

Moscow State University is another leading research facility in the area of brain-computer interfaces. In fact Dr. Alexander Kaplan, who designed the brain wave training algorithms that we use is the head of the Human Brain Research Group at Moscow State University and also heads the Moscow government project on stress diagnosis in elementary school and university students.

When you think about brain-based research we have some of the greatest minds in the world focusing their research on the question:

How we can re-pattern and rebalance the brain?

This research is being conducted in dozens of universities around the world right now because we're all living much longer and now we're faced with figuring out how to age gracefully. We want to have our memories intact and we want to maintain our concentration. We not only want to have a body that can function well into old age, but a sharp mind as well.

Biofeedback

Biofeedback is one of the early techniques that came out of research into how we can overcome stress symptoms and keep the brain fit. While that's basically the purpose of this book and the technology it describes, what we're talking about is not traditional, old-school biofeedback. While there's certainly a place for biofeedback, and great results can happen over time, the challenge is that it involves the conscious mind, not just the unconscious.

Biofeedback is conducted most often through mind challenges and games. Today, in addition to professional biofeedback therapy, there are several of these games on the market. In fact, last Christmas the fastest growing games on the market were brain-based games for children, which we were very excited to see.

The great thing is that Dr. Kaplan developed the dry sensor technology that went into those games along with neuro-tech guru Paul Donner, who is closely associated with us. They created an algorithm that teaches the brain to use brain waves to control or move objects, which is what we mean when we're talking about the brain-computer interface. There are many new mind technologies like this being developed on the market. Only recently have we been able to see brain waves as more than just squiggly lines on an EEG machine.

What's amazing is that almost universally the scientists conducting brain research are doing a great job of defining what the problem is, but are offering few if any real solutions to the problem.

This is where we come in; we're going to fill that void.

Conditioned Hyper-Eating

The former commissioner of the FDA, who once led the government's attack on addictive cigarettes, recently published research suggesting that millions of Americans suffer from conditioned hyper-eating, a willpower-sapping drive to eat—especially high-fat, high-sugar, salt-laden foods—even when not hungry. This condition occurs in the brain where these foods light up the brain's dopamine (pleasure-sensing) pathway—the same pathway that conditions people to alcohol or drugs. The research suggests that the food industry may be largely at fault for manipulating ingredients to stimulate our appetites, setting in motion a cycle of desire and consumption that has ended with a nation of overeaters who researchers say must "retrain their brains to resist the lure."

While these findings certainly help us to understand why diets fail, they do nothing to correct the ingrained (conditioned) eating habits that caused the weight problem in the first place. If the problem started in the brain, then we must change the brain to get lasting results. The brain-based wellness technology we're describing here is proven to naturally stimulate the brain's pleasure-sensing pathways, thus derailing conditioned hyper-eating. This is why one of the many programs you can offer using this technology is weight-loss. Your patients will learn to easily lose weight and keep it off because they change their whole relationship with food, mentally as well as physically.

Our patients have already been getting the results that we're talking about here. This new science of brain-based wellness is going to help you not only grow your practice but also set you up with a reputation that you are the new paradigm to health and wellness care because increasingly people want to find the solution for themselves, and not in a packet of pills.

They also want to find a solution that is readily available and accessible to their whole family. In fact self-care is one of the largest growing markets in health care at the moment.

"I'm 170 Lbs. Lighter!"

Randy Clusiau BEFORE SMT

Randy AFTER SMT

Randy Clusiau
Toronto, Ontario

My weight dropped from an obese 350 lbs. to an athletic 180 thanks to Dr. Patrick Porter's brain-based wellness program. That's 9 pant sizes! Most importantly, I've kept it off for four years!

I'd been overweight my entire adult life. I gained 100 lbs. between the ages of 20 and 25 and kept gaining. On airplanes I had to borrow the demo seatbelt just to buckle myself in. I've tried every crazy diet, fad, pill, gimmick and read the self-help books. The low-carb diet seemed great at first. As soon as I had one piece of bread, though, I was done. I was 32 years old and if I didn't change, I was going to have a heart attack before age 40. I needed to start by fixing the way I thought.

Instant Improvement!

I started Dr. Porter's program as my New Year's resolution at the beginning of 2008. Instantly, I slept better at night and my habits started changing. I drank a lot more water without thinking about it. After listening to an audio session, I'd go to the fridge and automatically be drawn to the fruits and vegetables.

I lost weight like crazy that first year. Even when the weight loss slowed, my changes continued. I haven't been this light since I was 17! I'm so stoked!

Brain-Based Wellness Makes All the Difference

I'd been eating to cope with stress, but now I've found new ways to cope. I have a well-balanced lifestyle now. The MindFit light and sound system is an amazing tool; I love listening to the sessions. It's my time to unplug from the world, to focus on me, relax and lower my stress level. When you're super relaxed and focused, everything sinks in and you're able to solve your problems.

I've been able to reprogram my brain so the way I look at food and the way I look at life are different. That's why I'm confident I'm going to keep my weight off for good.

Providing Patients an Experience

Now of course there are lots of self-help brain training techniques out there, the brain-training website Lumosity being one that we mentioned earlier, but the reality is that these games typically work only on cognition using old technology and techniques such as rote memorization. We can dramatically enhance the results of this conscious brain training by building on these techniques with neurosensory algorithms. We're going to talk a little bit about this later and just make sure it's clear that these algorithms go beyond words, it's more of a sensation or a feeling.

This is another aspect that makes brain-based wellness perfectly aligned with chiropractic care. When you're giving your patients an adjustment and creating outstanding clinical results, the patient is getting an experience, and it's the experience that makes a big difference to them. By shifting their breathing, physiology and focus, we help them achieve a peak state. They experience immediate results and feel cared for. This is what separates us from medical doctors. We're not just giving them a pill, and they're coming back weeks later to tell us how they feel. As a chiropractor, you can usually tell if what you're doing is having a result right then and there.

The same is true of brain-based wellness. For example, the binaurals work by the device sending one signal into one ear, and another into the other. So, for example, if we wanted to create an alpha state, and this is of course only one of the frequencies, we could put a 200 Hz frequency in the right ear and a 210 Hz frequency in the left ear; the brain then literally synchronizes the difference, which is 10 cycles (alpha) because that is the difference between the two.

This means, however, that binaurals are not all that effective for those who don't have full hearing range on both sides. For this reason, we've now included a new technology called isochronic tones. This works on a mono level so you don't have to have equal hearing in the ears; it works on a frequency response.

So to explain that a little bit more, the brain, as we've already discussed, works on varying levels of frequencies. For example if you were to travel from the UK to the US, you end up crossing several different time zones, which puts the body out of frequency, causing jet lag. Now part of this is due to the changes in light frequency, but it's more down to the fact that the world is resonating at different frequencies at different places and we tap into those frequencies. Research has found that our brains and bodies will synch to certain tones or frequencies, the isochronic tones.

This links with part of the research done by Dr. Kaplan on what he calls neuro-acoustic harmonics. His research has shown that we can take certain pieces of music and tune the music so that it is just off frequency. By doing this, we can trigger different parts of the brain; this is what the MindFit device is designed to do. We all know that the different parts of the brain control and focus different parts of our personality as well as memory, concentration, and focus to name but a few.

Throughout the session, the device is educating parts of your brain, not with words as we hopefully are doing right now, but with different acoustic harmonics; different harmonics cause the different areas of the brain to light up accordingly. So if someone were to take a picture of your brain while you were using the device, you would be able to pinpoint which parts of the brain were affected by which frequencies.

Recently, at multiple Masters Circle seminars, Dr. Richard Barwell used his NeuroInfiniti instrument, which documents brain wave patterns, to show how the MindFit system quickly and consistently rebalanced and harmonized the brain wave patterns of a member of the audience.

We can also use thermo imaging to see the increased blood flow to various parts of the brain as we trigger them and educate them. Now the great thing is that once all this happens, we create the relaxation response. When you're in this pleasurable state, your achievement levels go up and it doesn't feel like work anymore. So once your brain is in balance, it creates a euphoric feeling that keeps you active, energized and you can handle criticism much better if it shows up.

Can we really add $50,00 to the bottom line?

Now we're going to get down to the statistics. We titled this chapter, "How to add $50 thousand, $100 thousand or more to your bottom-line" for a reason.

If you were able to enroll just five patients per day to use Self-Mastery Technology for four days a week in your office, and each patient were to pay $50 per session, you would be able to generate $1000 a week in net profit. If you were to continue this for a year, you'll end up with $50,000 by the end of the year and, obviously, for every further five patients you add to your roster, you're going to add an additional $50,000 a year.

So if you were to have 10 people per day using Self-Mastery

Technology you would be collecting $2000 a week or $100,000 a year. When you consider that each session you do with a patient lasts just 20 minutes this really has to be considered as a great investment, that not only benefits you but your patients as well.

There are over 30 different programs to choose from, and later in the chapter we're going to go into details of the top five, but for the moment, let's just consider one of the top five, which is designed to help stressed patients.

Do you have five patients who are stressed out, that you could have sit in a comfortable chair for 20 minutes for a $50 cash fee? Imagine what would happen if you can help them rebalance, rev down, relax or go into that relaxation response that we talked about just a couple of paragraphs earlier where we're able to recreate the frequency and the vibration of the brain wave patterns that synchronize and create a state of homeostasis between the sympathetic and parasympathetic. It really is an amazing process.

Now before we dig any deeper we should address one of the questions you might be having, which is: Where would I do this? We've been to hundreds of chiropractic practices and in almost every one there has been some usable room. Perhaps what is currently in use as the closet or junk room could accommodate one or two comfortable chairs where you could have your patients sitting back and relaxing. We'll discuss this more as we get to the implementation phase. If you don't have an extra room, don't worry, it doesn't mean that you can't implement this program.

At this point, you shouldn't be thinking about tying up the adjusting room, but if nothing else you could have patients do this in the reception room. It's certainly not ideal but it is a workable model because the patients are tuned into the headphones and glasses and are unaware of other people around them, and it will not affect the result. Not only that, you'll have the curiosity factor at play. When your new patients come in, they'll see other patients looking wonderfully relaxed and will ask to give it a try.

We've found that in most practices there are numerous ways Self-Mastery Technology can be implemented. Consider that each session lasts for only 20 minutes, therefore, you could do two people in an hour with just one station, but you could have more stations if you have the space, and that's when the possibilities could be huge.

But even if you see just five people per day at $50 per session for an average of four days a week, that's $1000 per week net profit. This really is a very simple, yet profound business model that could have a massive impact on your practice.

We're going to discuss this further later on in this chapter but for now we just want to make it clear that you don't have to purchase anything, but if you do then you do have options; how to set this up, where to do it. Keep in mind that your staff can implement almost the entire system.

This new side of your business should not take away from your existing practice, you'll be getting a lot of new patients, going through your regular adjusting protocols and your adjusting visits will grow. If you focus on that, then your chiropractic practice will grow simultaneously with this side of the business.

The great part of this as a business model is that you only pay once for the technology, it's not like a renewable business where you have to keep adding into it. Once you've made your original investment that's it, and you will find that your original investment will soon have paid for itself.

This is yet another reason why we are convinced that Self-Mastery Technology is totally congruent and consistent with chiropractic care and the chiropractic philosophy. Every adjustment reboots and defrags the brain; so does Self-Mastery Technology. For all chiropractic techniques, the common denominator, the reason that they all work together, is because they're all working with the brain and the nervous system; and again the same is true for the Self-Mastery Technology. The connection between the two is extremely strong.

Top 5 systems that we would recommend

Now we're going to get into the top 5 systems to help people de-stress and heal from the inside-out.

So, of course the number one program, especially within our chiropractic business, has got to be the pain-free lifestyle program. People are often initially drawn to a chiropractor because they are seeking some relief from pain, or perhaps they are having adjustments done to prevent the pain in the first place. Either way their main purpose for seeking out chiropractic care is to have a pain-free life.

Number two would have to be the stress-free program, As we've already discussed, this is a program that again almost all chiropractic patients are in need of at one point or another.

Weight loss is another thing that many people are striving for in our modern world. Statistics have shown that only 10 percent of the American population will see a chiropractor at some point in their life, but 93 percent of the population is not happy with their weight, so that's a huge untapped client base.

Smoking is another big problem, although not as prevalent as it was say ten years ago, there are still millions of smokers, and a large number of people attempt to quit or at least want to be free of their habit. The pain and the symptoms that come with withdrawal are what put off the greater percentage of these people.

Lastly, there is a large percentage of the population who suffer from some form of sleep disorder. One of the things that you will find, as we did, is that around 50 percent of your patients will come back after the first demo session and tell you that they had, "The best night's sleep they've ever had," after the session. We created the Insomnia relief program specifically for these patients.

One of the things that we really want to emphasize here is that these are just five of over 30 programs that have been created. These

30 programs are split into two categories; you've got the programs that help to address a condition, as these given are, and others that are about promoting wellness. So for example, without going through the whole system, you've got programs on life mastery, menopause, winning relationships, vibrant health, wealth accumulation and accelerated learning. We believe these programs are really important weapons in our arsenal to be able to help people and to target prospective patients for the practice.

The great thing is that we've only mentioned a small portion of the programs available to you here but you are free to pick whatever program, or programs you want, and these programs are not limited, we are coming up with new ones to add to our inventory all the time. Again, you don't necessarily have to have all 32 of the programs, you can have just one, five or ten. Pick what resonates with you, what you find to be a pressing issue for you and your community. You could even just start with one and then build up your program as your client base and demand grows. That's the key to this whole program, it's not just about equipping you with more knowledge, it's about utilizing the technology to help people and to help yourself to generate a new stream of income, and generate new reasons for people to start and continue to care.

One thing that you might be interested to know is that we have marketing tools designed specifically to help you in setting this technology up in your existing business. We have in-house marketing, and the external marketing set up specifically to help you. We know that it's important for you to not only have a good product in your clinic, but you also need to drive in new patients as well; we're going to discuss this more in Chapter 6.

Pain-Free Program

Let's start by discussing the pain-free program; we've designed some posters as you can see below. Of course you have to imagine this with your logo on it. Using a poster like this will allow you to inform your patients that you have a new program. Obviously, with the

picture on the right you've got the patient there on the front and then you've got the same patient using the equipment on the right hand side. An important aspect of the marketing is that the poster and the leaflet were designed and written by a world-class copywriter; she's trained with some of the top people, including Jay Abraham and Dan Kennedy.

We've done a lot of research on the marketing side of the program and we've looked into the knowledge that the patient needs to read to get them to respond and take action. So we'll give you these flyers at cost from Vista Print, it's all ready and set up for you it just needs you to plug in, put your name and address in there and then this becomes your own in-house flyer.

What we do at our own clinic is we rotate through the top 5 programs that we've mentioned here, so that we have a different one each week on display. We find that it helps to turn conversation in the clinic towards the program because the patients will always notice it when they're waiting for their appointments, even more so if it's a different poster each week.

So, for example, let's say that this week we're featuring pain control. We'll have everyone in the office talking about the pain control program. We have them informing people what's involved in the program or what's available and then we let them have a listen to one of the demo sessions so that they can have an understanding of what the program is all about.

The recommended program is 12 weeks, but at the end of the day it can be adjusted to what works best for you. We tend to do the relaxation techniques before we do the adjustment, we find that it's the best time and it makes for easier adjustments. But there is no reason why you can't do it the other way around so that you have them listen to the SMT after the adjustment. Either way, the basics of the program will be the same and that means that every time they come into the clinic they're going to have an adjustment and an SMT session. And, because there are multiple sessions within each series, you're going to have a different session for them to listen to at each visit.

Now we haven't mentioned yet why the program is 12 weeks long and again it has been specifically designed this way to have maximum effect. Stanford University conducted a study that showed it takes 18 months to make a life change at the conscious level. More importantly, they found that relaxation-visualization techniques reduced that timeframe to only 21 days. Now most people, especially in today's fast-paced society who are accustomed to instant results, believe that the study showed that 21 days is all the time it takes to form a new habit, and they forget about the relaxation-visualization part of the equation.

So what we need to do is to re-train or re-pattern the way that we think about our lives and we've found that 12 weeks seems to be the perfect amount of time for our patients to really be able to evaluate their life, what it was like before and what they need to do so that they can become stress and pain free.

An important concept for you to understanding in regard to relieving pain is that our brains only perceive pain when in beta mode. Once the brain shifts into a better balance of alpha and theta, the pain response diminishes considerable. This is why the brain-based wellness program is key to your success as a pain relief practitioner – the system works by shifting brain waves out of beta and into alpha and theta. No other pain relief method—including drugs—has this capability.

This is why we strongly urge you to provide your patients a

complimentary SMT session. You will find that 99 out of 100 people will finish that first session feeling so refreshed and revitalized that they can't help but want to come back. It's so easy to sign people up because they feel an immediate improvement.

We have our patients coming in twice a week for a session, so they complete the whole 12-session series within six weeks. We have some doctors who have clients on the program and they only have their patients coming in once a week, so for them it takes 12 weeks to complete the program.

We've found that having the patient coming in twice a week has a better effect because we have the residual benefit of using the SMT and we find that it tends to last around two to three days before it starts to wear off. They can get results from listening once a week of course, but we find that you get the best results from participating in the program twice a week.

In total there are 13 different pain sessions. Each one uses a different neuro-linguistic process designed to train their brains to better process information, because pain is essentially information signals being sent to the brain. So we're looking at getting them through the adjustments and then this program is aimed at getting them back to working more efficiently and effectively once they leave the office and go about their daily lives, so they stay pain free.

We've been working on this for quite some time and we've worked out a formula of what we think is the perfect list of nutritional support to give to your patients in order to assist them in getting and staying healthy. Now of course we're aware that, as a chiropractor, nutrition is something that is personal to you, and you will most likely have your own ideas about the perfect nutritional support, so we're not going to say this is what you must do, we're just giving you an idea of what we personally have found to work the best for our patients. The list below takes into account just some of the nutritional supplements that you can get and there are loads of different vendors out there to get them from. We recommend using doctor's only brands because we find that doctor's only brands will provide your patients with more benefit, especially since most don't know the difference between synthetic and whole-food vitamins.

We're going to get further into this in later chapters and how you can build up your own range of supplements and increase sales through your practice. In fact, our practice sells as much as $10,000 a week worth of supplements, so there's definitely a huge market out there. So as long as you're getting those doctor's supplements out there, you're going to be doing a great service to your patients, as well as increasing your own bottom line.

Pain-free Supplementation From Solutions4

- Anti-Inflammatory
- Antioxidant
- Appetite Appeaser
- Body Purifier
- Digestive Enzyme blend
- Evening Primrose Oil
- Flax Seed Oil
- Fiber Blend
- Intestinal Cleanser
- Joint & Muscle Relief
- Liquid Calcium
- Multivitamin - Multimineral
- Nutritional Shake
- Probiotic Blend
- Vitamin D
- Herbal Stress Relief

We also advise our patients on using physical exercise to help maintain their health but of course this is up to the overseeing doctor to arrange with the patient at the time of examination. They might decide to give them certain exercises based on the fact that when neurons fire together they wire together. We're discussing how to do this manually with a combination of physical exercise and nutrition that will get the brain to start wiring and reprogramming itself to bring the body back to health.

Another important statistic for you is that 47 percent of Americans report at least one of the three types of chronic pain; again this is completely unacceptable, especially when we can do something about it.

Stress-Free Program

The second program we're going to be looking at is the stress-free program. We've found that stress is a moving target because people are often stressed, but don't do anything about it. They tend to ignore stress most of the time, which makes the problem worse. For example, if you were to go out there shouting to anyone who will listen that you have the solution to becoming stress free, chances are that you wouldn't get many takers because most people fail to acknowledge that they're stressed. Nobody wants to admit to themselves or those around them that they can't manage stress and need help.

What we find is that when we run stress seminars and teach people about how stress is affecting their bodies, they start to confide in you. Once you get them to start talking about stress and some of the symptoms of stress they start to realize that yes, that does apply to me; I am stressed.

So you're in a perfect position to change the lives of the patients coming through your clinic for your chiropractic care. Maybe they've already moved away from the pain phase, but they're still in need of some maintenance, which is the perfect time to introduce the stress program. They need to learn how to handle and manage stress so the pain doesn't return, just as we discussed at the very beginning of this chapter. Again they might not even know that they're under stress, but you're in the position to make them understand that they are under stress and that this is part of the reason why they were in pain in the first place; all too often they have no idea why their body is behaving the way it is and it's up to us to make them understand why.

In the stress program, we provide titles that involve putting future events into perspective and organizing your day, because, as you know, you have some patients who can't even handle taking a vacation. People need to start somewhere, and perhaps that's just learning to set time aside to let their minds expand and relax the way we used to as children, to really engage those alpha and theta brain wave patterns.

Of course, we recommend that you combine this with nutritional support. It's surprising how many people still don't even bother to take a good multivitamin, and they still don't understand why they have no energy or are not sleeping well.

Some people will turn to the pharmaceutical option and they think that they're getting rid of stress, but in reality all they're doing is masking the symptoms of stress. In fact one-third of all US employees are chronically overworked. In our clinic we sell not only the program at $50 per session, but we put together a whole package including all of the supplements that we're talking about here in this book.

For our stress-free and pain-free programs for example, the program in our clinic sells for $1077. So once we include all the supplements in the program, our cost comes to around $130.

We coach our patients every two weeks just as you are probably being coached by The Master Circle or a mentor of some kind while you're building your practice. Just as you need a coach for your business, your patients need a coach to help them to achieve the changes that they're setting out to make by embarking on one of our programs. So you can be the coach, or you could always train some of your staff to be the coach, whatever works best for you. With our coaching, we teach our patients some very basic skills that they can utilize to help them keep their progress on track and on target.

So now your program price went up from $50 to over $100, because you're adding your expertise into the program as well. Again it's up to you how you decide to work it; you can always just keep doing the SMT for $50, or you can package these programs along with your expertise. If you can get four or five people to sign up to these all-inclusive packages, then you're looking at achieving an added income of around $5000 a week instead of just $1000.

Stress-Free Supplementation from Solutions4

- Antioxidant
- Appetite Appeaser
- Body Purifier
- Digestive Enzyme Blend
- Evening Primrose Oil
- Flax Seed Oil
- Fiber Blend
- Intestinal Cleanser
- Liquid Calcium
- Herbal Stress Relief
- Multivitamin -Multimineral
- Nutritional Shake
- Probiotic Blend
- Vitamin D

Emotional Eating Program

The third program that we're going to look at is the Emotional Eating Program. Again many people wanting to achieve some amount of weight loss will turn to pharmaceutical options such as appetite suppressants to help them in their endeavor. Now they may be somewhat successful on this regime while they are taking the drug, but what happens once they stop? The reality is that they will more than likely see the weight creeping back on again because they are just going back to their old habits; nothing has changed in their mindset. We have created 54 different sessions to help people with weight loss.

Now we've been telling you that all of our programs are 12-week programs, but this program can be extended to a full one-year program if needed. And today we're seeing more and more people with 75 to 100 or more pounds to lose, and these folks need that ongoing support.

The patient will come in every week and listen to something different; we've made it 54 so that you can also have the holidays in there when most people overindulge in food. For example, we have one week entitled, Have Your Turkey and Lose Weight" for during Thanksgiving and we have Holiday Weight Loss which we use during the week between Christmas and New Year's, getting our patients ready and geared up for New Year's Resolutions.

Again we promote this program throughout our clinics. We use posters and leaflets, which get rotated with the other four main programs that we have to offer. You could quite easily generate the kind of traffic that we've been talking about purely by having these leaflets and posters in your practice, and just getting the walk-in traffic.

Something that we think is unique about this program, and that makes it so great and effective, is that we've added a success coaching element to it. What we've found with the weight loss program is that we have to get them in and speak to them; you have to do a little hand-holding.

Have you ever wondered why Weight Watchers is so successful as a business and why their members continue to attend meetings? Well, the short answer is because people have the chance to communicate, they can discuss the journey with someone else and this has a huge impact on the final outcome, that's why we've decided to include coaching here.

At the end of the first 12 weeks, they can sign up for another 12 weeks and then another 12 weeks until they've gone through the whole year. Some people will actual stay with you and go through the whole course again. We've got one lady who's been with us for three years now. She's lost over 70 pounds but she still wants to continue because of the support she gets.

So as an example of a complete weight loss package, they're going to get the weight loss adjustment as we call it, which means that we're going to be getting their body and neurology working in harmony together so that they can burn fat faster and more efficiently. We're going to give them the success coaching and we're going to give them relaxation sessions as well, with each of them being different. We also have the nutritional support element that we talked about, not only the supplements themselves but also the classes to address the patient's knowledge of the supplements that they should be taking. We want to educate them to be naturally thin people and again we're going to get them to use their physiology to activate the part of their brain that really need to make this change work for them.

We're going to give you the supplement list for the weight loss program and you will notice on this one that the focus is on cleansing. We put our patients on a 20-day cleanse and we've had an average weight loss for our patients of about 15 pounds. These results are very similar to those of hCG but the difference is that our patients don't have to starve themselves. They're eating real food, cleansing their bodies and getting their brains in balance so that they can get thin and stay thin naturally for the rest of their lives.

Weight Loss Supplementation from Solutions4

- Antioxidant
- Appetite Appeaser
- Body Purifier
- Digestive Enzyme Blend
- Evening Primrose Oil
- Flax Seed Oil
- Fiber Blend
- Intestinal Cleanser
- Liquid Calcium
- Herbal Stress Relief
- Multivitamin - Multimineral
- Nutritional Shake
- Probiotic Blend
- Vitamin D

Stop Smoking

Some of you may have heard of me (Patrick Porter) before and you will know that I started my own stop smoking clinics back in the 80s. Business was booming to start with, but in the end so many people had quit that it was no longer viable to have a practice that only dealt with non-smoking.

We've had such great success with our stop smoking program and it fits in really well with your already existing practice. Most of our patients will just come in, we'll do a little coaching, they'll listen to the program and they will stop smoking within the program parameters. If you've got a patient who smokes more than two packs per day, then we also put them on a cleanse alongside the anti-smoking program.

There are 46.6 million smokers in the US, with a further 88 million non-smokers that are exposed to second hand smoke all the time. The chances are that even if your patient is not a smoker, he or she will know someone who is. Invite those folks in for a demo session. We let our patients listen to the first smoking session before they join and we find that they will cut back on their cigarette intake right away. You'll have them convinced. You'll have them coming back in and they'll be saying, "Last week I was smoking twenty cigarettes and now I'm only smoking ten."

Again, it's a 12 week program; they're going to come in and get an adjustment because we need their physiology and their psychology to match. The same as with the weight loss program, we've added a mentoring section to the non-smoking program. People need to talk to someone about their smoking addiction along with taking part in the program. We've found that if there isn't somebody one-on-one helping them along the way, encouraging them to get rid of all their smoking paraphernalia, they continue to procrastinate. They just need that bit of encouragement. Weight loss clients and stop smoking clients are really great at procrastinating; they just need someone to give them a little push now and then.

The nice thing about the Stop Smoking program is that you're teaching them how to relax and solve their problems so that they won't need to rely on the cigarettes anymore when things get tough. They're also going to be in need of a lot of nutritional support because we've found that most smokers really don't take their health seriously. You'll find that there are a small group of smokers out there who manage to convince themselves, if no one else, that they really are healthy but the majority are aware that they aren't.

In our clinic we have the vibration exercise machine that we use with our smoking patients. The full-body vibration helps to advance the detox process. We have the 20-day detox for heavy smokers, and we also have a 9-day cleanse as well; so there are different cleanses that they can do to purify their body. So we've got the supplements that they take, the personal SMT sessions and the coaching.

Stop Smoking Supplementation from Solutions4

- Antioxidant
- Appetite Appeaser
- Body Purifier
- Digestive Enzyme Blend
- Evening Primrose Oil
- Flax Seed Oil
- Fiber Blend
- Intestinal Cleanser
- Liquid Calcium
- Herbal Stress Relief
- Multivitamin - Multimineral
- Nutritional Shake
- Probiotic Blend
- Vitamin D

Insomnia

The last program that we're going to discuss is the Insomnia Program. The insomnia program that we have is a shorter program but we've found that people who have problems with insomnia also need to deal with stress; so we decided to marry the two together.

The Insomnia program is a 5-week program, but once they've finished the insomnia program we then re-enroll them onto the stress program. People will get great results with the insomnia program and they will want to come back and do the stress program as well. Around 70 percent of the people that take the initial insomnia program will enroll in another program after they're done.

When you think about it, before the invention of electricity, adults would typically sleep more than ten hours a night, today the average is just six. In fact, around half of adults today, as soon as we tell them about SMT, they say, "Wow, I need that because I don't sleep well at night."

This is typical of today's population, and it's due to the fact that they're brains are not fit, they really need to re-train their brains to enter into those deep sleep cycles. So again, we're going to take them through the chiropractic adjustment sessions alongside the success coaching, these can be done during most of our programs. You don't necessarily need a second person for this. While you're doing the adjustments you can do a little bit of coaching, getting their outcomes, keeping them focused on the results and giving them nutritional support.

Now with the insomnia program, the nutrition side is a little bit different because they need certain things to be able to get their bodies back into balance and most of the clients that we see are also on medication. We don't tell patients to get off their medication for obvious reasons, but we do advise them to go to the prescribing doctor who can devise a program to help them wean themselves off, because they're not going to need as much once they start working through the program.

Insomnia Supplementation from Solutions4

- Antioxidant
- Appetite Appeaser
- Body Purifier
- Digestive Enzyme Blend
- Evening Primrose Oil
- Flax Seed Oil
- Fiber Blend
- Intestinal Cleanser
- Liquid Calcium
- Herbal Stress Relief
- Multivitamin / Multimineral
- Nutritional Shake
- Probiotic Blend
- Vitamin D

Taking Action

The assignment for this chapter is for you to think about which program or programs you want to roll out first and start a pilot program. We want you to do a test. Choose any of the topics and get people to come in for a complimentary session. Perhaps start with some of your regular chiropractic clients who know you well and trust your judgment. Once you start to see the amazing results following our protocols, we're confident that you'll want to add more programs and really start pushing it out to other areas of your practice. Start with a simple program and build from there.

We're going to ask you to start changing the conversations within your practice; make appointments to speak to your patients around the topics that you've selected to start with. So for example, if you've decided to start with the insomnia program, go through your active patient list and see which of your patients you know to have sleep problems. Once you've done that, sit them down and have a heart-to-heart conversation.

We recommend that you introduce SMT with the simplest of steps—offering a demonstration. The critical part of the demo, however, is for you to pre-frame the patient. In other words, get the patient to have a positive expectation before they even begin.

Pre-Framing SMT for an Existing Patient

Start the conversation by stating:

Chiropractic care has been instrumental in helping to prevent deterioration from the bombardment of constant stress. But I've come across an amazing new technology that, in conjunction with chiropractic adjustments, will allow you to make significant and continuous progress in getting well in spite of the stress.

Here is an alternative paragraph...

As a result of your chiropractic care, you are now making significant progress where your brain and body are communicating far more effectively. You are ready for the second stage in your healing where we use the latest technology to help balance your brain and help you neutralize stress and heal at a faster pace.

Next say to the patient:

I'd like for you to do a test with this new technology. It's a simple 10 or 20-minute test...it's painless...and at the end of the test I will know based on how you respond if you will thrive and flourish with this program as most people do, or if you're one of the 1 or 2% I shouldn't be recommending it to.

So all you'll need to do is close your eyes and relax. There are three common responses that I am looking for that will signal to me that this addition to your care program will dramatically help you thrive, heal and recover. Most patients will either fall asleep or at the end of the trial feel very relaxed, centered, calm and peaceful...the second most common response is the opposite where at the end you will feel totally focused, energized and reinvigorated...and, the third and by far least common response is feeling slightly spacey for a few minutes. Any of these kinds of sensations are a positive test that this technology, in addition to your chiropractic adjustments, will absolutely speed up your healing, help you completely neutralize life stress, and become healthy, vital and well again.

And then you let the patient do the SMT demonstration.

Providing the demo is key to your success because of the very real benefits the patients receive. They feel more balanced, more relaxed, and are more available for your recommendation than ever before.

Once the patient has the positive responses that you pre-framed them with, say the following: *(98 out of 100 patients will have a positive test trial.)*

Great, now that this has been a positive test, let's sit down and

I want to tell you what I'm recommending and why.

It takes an average person about 12 weeks to create the necessary rewiring and rebalancing of their brain. And it will take 2 sessions a week in order to make that happen in that timeframe.

We suggest is that you don't do this in a democratic fashion. Let the patient know that doing this technology in addition to their chiropractic care is essential, necessary, and important. Don't ask bad questions like, "Are you okay with this?" or "Do you want to give this a try?" You are the doctor, so tell the patient why you are recommending SMT training and why it is important to their health; then assume the close.

The money is negotiable if necessary, but their health is not negotiable. In other words, doing this versus not doing this is not negotiable. Neuro-training is now a part of your care. Now what I mean about money being negotiable is this: I'm not willing to necessarily reduce the price that much further, but what I am willing to do is allow them to either pay me up front, or they could pay me half now and the other half in six weeks. Or they can even pay it weekly if they needed to. It comes out to $85 to $100 a week. I'm available for all those different options…what I'm not available for is them not accepting my recommendation.

Pre-Framing for a New Patient

You will recommend the SMT neuro-training program at the report of findings, keeping in mind that you are repositioning chiropractic to the new patient: Chiropractic is not about relieving nerve pressure; it's about creating brain balance.

Start the conversation by stating:

Based on your case history, your examination, your lifestyle decisions, coupled with my experience, I'm going to be recommending two different facets of care that work together synergistically and that will get us the best, fastest, and longest lasting results. I'm going to recommend your chiropractic care as follows... (Here's where you recommend, the certain number of chiropractic visits over a specific length of time). ...And I'm going to recommend MindFit neuro-training twice a week in order to help balance your brain, because regaining health is all about normalizing and maximizing brain function. The adjustment does that, and so does the MindFit system. If we do both together, we are going to get the best, fastest, and longest-lasting results.

No matter which program you have elected to begin with, we want you to work out how many patients you could be helping with this program. If for example, you're seeing 20 people a day, you should have little problems in having at least five of them try this program, and that would generate you an extra $50,000 a year. If you're seeing 40, 50 or 60 people a day, there's no reason why you can't get 10, 12 or even 20 people a day to try this program. So the number of people you can get in to try the program each day is largely dependent on the size of your current practice, your commitment to building up your client list, and having a proper plan to help you target your patients.

Evaluate your action plans for your own personal brain health; this is an extremely important step in your plan. Once you tell your patients that you use the technology and that it's had an amazing impact on your life, it will really help you to sell the product to them. We also encourage you to have your entire staff do regular neuro-training as well so they can effectively communicate the benefits to your patients.

Resources Available to You

Before we end this chapter, it's really important for us to just go through some of the options that you have available to you. There is no need for you to purchase anything. If you just decided to undertake the nutrition, the chiropractic adjustments and the exercise, then you will start to see some significant changes in some of your patients. For those doctors who want to see even more dramatic changes there are options to invest in.

We're going to start from the top down in terms of levels of commitment and investment.

The first option is for someone who maybe has a larger space to do this in, we offer a Classroom Model Location License program where we can put five people on the same SMT session at a time, so you can run your own classes. This is what we'd call the "Cadillac program." It comes complete with an iPod touch with the entire library loaded on it, all of the sessions, which is over 500 sessions, with all 30 programs at your fingertips ready to use. It also comes complete with five of our MindFit Neuro-Trainer light-and-sound machines.
The second level Location License program is what we call the business-builder package. It includes an iPod with everything that you need to run your practice, and to start introducing people to the program. It comes complete with five of our MindFit Neuro-Trainer light-and-sound machines and an iPod touch loaded with the entire library. This is where most people start. They'll start putting people on SMT sessions, and they'll resell those other Mind Fit machines for $395 each to their patients.

The third location license program, which we've designed as a less expensive alternative is a Limited Location License. We'll give you an IPod Nano with six programs, the five that we talked about in this chapter and the Learning Series. You'll get three MindFit devices, one to use in your clinic and two to sell to your patients if they want to use it at home. Each time you sell one of the MindFit units to your clients you're going to be making $395 (recommended retail); so if you sell both units then you're getting the whole program for $210.

Now the fourth program that we have is for those people who prefer to start with a single unit for personal own use. For $395 you will get 16 sessions, along with 10 sessions that we recorded for our brain-based wellness webinar. So you're getting 26 sessions in total along with the Mind Fit unit.

So again you can start at whatever level suits your budget but you should get started.

*For further details, call our HELP DESK at 800-901-4980

CHAPTER
FIVE

Incorporating Brain-Based Wellness for Quicker and More Sustainable Clinical Outcomes

Incorporating Brain-Based Wellness for quicker and more sustainable clinical outcomes

This chapter is going to focus on providing you information on the untapped markets of the chiropractic world. We're going to marry together the two aspects of Brain-Based Wellness in the process of weight loss to show you how you can maximize your office space and profitability.

Natural, healthy, sustainable weight loss is a huge market in today's society. In this chapter we're going to show you why and we're also going to show you how brain imbalance contributes to body imbalance and weight imbalance and how to utilize the Brain-Based Wellness system to add weight loss to your clinic's services.

We're going to start by putting weight loss in the context of chiropractic. Statistics show around 9 to 11 percent of the population in the US is using a chiropractor, this is obviously a small percentage and that's why we're talking here about expanding into the weight loss market, which is much larger. In fact, being overweight has surpassed smoking as the highest number of preventable deaths in the US today. Two thirds of adults are overweight with one third of those being obese. With so many weight loss management programs out there, what's going wrong? Why are they not having a bigger impact? If we're looking at the statistics over time, we see the percentage of overweight population in the US keeps increasing, and it has reached epidemic proportions.

Now let's get down to some statistics again, we're going to show you a real life example of what's possible for you to achieve. We took over a California clinic in May of 2009, in the middle of what was supposedly a depression for the industry. We started out slowly and in that first month had done $20,000 in weight loss services. We steadily built it up and by month 5, we were at $129,000, and around 85 percent of our business is weight loss.

Needless to say, to make that kind of money, we had to invest in advertising, but we're confident that today you can get the same or better results, six to ten times return on your investment.

Why is this so important? Well, in most towns anyone looking for a chiropractor can almost throw a rock in any direction and hit a chiropractor. The same cannot be said for someone getting results in weight loss. In fact we've found that whatever market we've been to, there has never been any competition because there is no one out there addressing the mental and emotional sides of the equation, and no one else getting the kind of results in weight loss we are.

The average dieter ends up gaining weight instead of losing it, and most don't last past 72 hours. They start the diet on a Monday and give up by Wednesday. Over the weekend they eat all of the things they gave up during their diet and they start on the diet again on the following Monday. This habit turns into a vicious cycle.

The average American woman by the age of 50 has spent 31 years of her life on a diet. That's a shocking statistic that goes to show traditional and commercial weight loss programs are not working.

As a country, we've focused on the heal issues related to smoking, and there's been improvement to show for it. The number of adults smoking has dropped from 54 percent of the population in the 80s down to 19 percent today. It's still not where we'd ideally want it to be, but as we've already said, obesity has now overtaken smoking as the most preventable killer. With a growing epidemic on the horizon, and no viable method of dealing with it, chiropractors are perfectly positioned to provide a safe, natural, long-lasting solution.

We also have to remember that being obese leads to other healthcare conditions such as heart disease, diabetes and cancer. We also have to recognize that this issue of weight gain is a by-product of a few other issues; the first being that people are far more inactive than they have ever been before, with the invention of the computer and other technologies we can do pretty much everything at the touch of a button from our armchair. Our Western diets don't help the matter either. And we've already discussed how our overloaded lifestyles are to blame.

There are many weight loss programs out there, but none of

them produce consistent results. Why?

Because they are not getting to the root cause of the problem, to the real reason people are overeating and not exercising. They try to change people's diets instead of their minds. People start starving themselves and depriving themselves of the foods they want the most and within 72 hours they stop because they can't sustain it.

They want to exercise but they don't feel good and they don't have the motivation to do it because again they have not addressed the brain dysfunction that caused the problem in the first place. No one has helped them to neutralize the stress that led to the brain dysfunction in the first place; that's what we're going to look at now and how to deal with it.

Stress has an immense impact on our weight and, as we've already said, stress is the most pervasive malady of our time, the "silent killer." We've also discussed how 90 percent of all illness is stress related according to the National Institutes of Health.

The problem is stress might not always be felt as stress, but it can go straight to the body, affecting its weakest points. Finally we need to recognise that pain hurts, but stress kills. That's an important factor, and I know we keep saying it, but we want to drive home the connection for those of you reading this, not only for yourselves but for the sake of your patients and their health as well.

We're talking about taking it to the next level by getting the brain to work in harmony with the body, and the body to work with the brain. Once we achieve this harmony, people can learn to think, eat and act like a naturally thin person, thus helping them to lose weight and maintain that weight loss for life. When the brain and the body finally work in harmony, we can achieve great results in weight loss.

Why does stress have such an impact on our weight?

So let's discuss how stress sets all of this off. We have the fight-or-flight response, which leads to what we have referred to and labelled as Sympathetic Survival Syndrome. It has also recently been referred to as defense physiology, because the body is in defense mode. This system, as we are all aware, is a genetic development of the body designed to help keep us from harm. It's innate intelligence at work. Now remember innate intelligence is all about survival as well. So even though we are surviving through an innate process, genetic wisdom is working. The problem comes when we're not given the opportunity to wind down and relax. We're trapped in Sympathetic Survival Syndrome, and that's when we start to have some serious problems.

This is another reason why diet programs have poor results overall. Diets by their very nature follow the principle that you make decisions on a conscious level. But most of us don't have enough time on the conscious level to think about better eating choices, so under stress we revert back to our primitive behavior, or the fight-or-flight response.

Everyone starts out their diet with the best of intentions. They wake up in the morning with every intention of exercising and eating healthy. But then stress kicks in, someone brings a box of donuts to the office, and before they know it all the positive thinking and good intentions are out the window.

This is why Brain-Based Wellness is so effective, because it's about setting aside the time to relax and be conscious and aware of what's going on in your environment and the world around you. We need to create the future we prefer first in our minds, then let our body's settle and recover and start to believe it's possible. Then we can begin to live that truth out as we go through our day-to-day experiences. That's what Brain-Based Wellness is going to do for not only the doctors out there but for each of your patients who come through your program.

We have clients coming into the clinic all of the time and they tell me they're lifelong members of Weight Watchers. I ask them, "Why would you want to watch your weight for the rest of your life?" Wouldn't it be better to simply think like a naturally thin person? Because naturally thin people watch the food they consume but they don't watch their weight; they don't even usually weigh themselves.

They have an image in their mind of their body and the things that work together to create the physiological effects necessary.

So when you're getting the right supplementation, the right nutritional component and the right psychological component, along with physical activity, true and permanent weight loss happens. This is how we get people out of that lose/gain cycle, because they have to take action and change their lives.

So as we continue on with the discussion of the fight-or-flight response and sympathetic survival syndrome, we have to remember that too much fight-or-flight activity without the corresponding rest and relaxation is what distress is all about.

In today's fast paced, high-stress world, it's not good enough to take a one-minute break and expect your brain to go back into balance. It won't work that way, that easily or that quickly, so we're stuck in beta mode and our brain is racing. We've got to give our brains the opportunity to go into alpha and theta modes or where it can start to rev down the sympathetic nervous system and rev up the parasympathetic system until we get back to homeostasis.

We were at a seminar with Dr. Porter where we did a demonstration where we had somebody hooked up to the NeuroInfiniti machine and we were able to show people on a big 12-foot screen that he was trapped in a beta mode stress pattern. He was wide-awake, conscious and his nervous system was revved up. Then Dr Porter put the light and sound technology on him and within six minutes we could see the beta-wave pattern in his brain start to decrease. Soon the alpha and theta waves started to increase and he went into a relaxation response. After the session, he reported feeling, "relaxed and calm while at the same time wide-awake and alert."

During fight-or-flight, our adrenals go into overdrive. Most patients we see in our office have adrenal malfunction and adrenal exhaustion; this is why people are exhausted all the time. The chemicals they release to deal with stress, cortisol or adrenaline sets the body up for all kinds of serious problems.

When you're under stress and feeling exhausted, it doesn't necessarily mean you're not getting all of the right nutritional supplements. You can be getting all the nutrition you need, but the body isn't functioning at its highest level. So you need to give your body the best chance you can for the innate intelligence, the super-conscious awareness that's a natural part of the body to work with those nutritional supplements you might be taking or even the foods you're eating so you can metabolize, digest and use it for energy.

Adrenaline

We mentioned adrenaline very briefly. Adrenaline sends signals to the digestive system to decrease the activity of the stomach, primarily because digestion is not essential to immediate survival. Even though you might be taking all of the right supplements, if your body is in fight-or-flight most of the day, it won't be able to break those supplements down properly.

There's probably a good chance your adrenal glands are not working as efficiently and as effectively as necessary. It could have to do with the types of food you're consuming, but it could also have to do with the level of stress you're under. When you think about stress in relation to weight, you must understand that stress stimulates the hormones that regulate the body's desire for fat and carbohydrates. So when our clients come through our practice and they tell us they're having a great day, having fun, and doing things they enjoy, they usually also tell me they're eating well. When things go bad is when their eating choices go downhill. When they start getting stressed out, they reach for the candy bar, they reach for the sweets, because they want the sugar rush; they want to change their physiology by eating something unhealthy for their bodies.

Cortisol

When our cortisol level and blood sugar levels increase, insulin shoots up as well. For those of you unfamiliar with it, insulin is a fat-storage hormone. Insulin tells the body to stop burning fat because its job is to burn up the sugar in the bloodstream. Cortisol, being the survival hormone, programs the body to store fat for future famines.

Fat in small amounts is beneficial. It protects you by helping to keep toxins out of your bloodstream. The downside of cortisol is that it will tell your body to store fat in the places you least want it, like the belly, buttocks, arms, and thighs. This kind of adipose tissue can be hard to get rid of once you create it. We've had patients come in and say, "I'm running two to three miles a day and still not losing weight." This is because all that running is probably stressing out an already overburdened body. To lose weight for life, you have to strike a healthy balance between healthy foods, exercise and relaxation. Unfortunately, there are dozens of exercise programs that overwork and stress out the body, causing weight gain instead of loss.

Cortisol also increases the body's tendency to burn protein rather than fat. This is bad because your resting metabolic rate is now being altered. This means when the body is at rest it burns a certain number of calories each day. Protein burns the most calories when you are at rest. If you're taking away the protein (muscle) from the equation, your metabolic rate has now gone down as well. This is what happens through most diet programs. People eat too few calories for sustaining their activity level, which prompts a stress (cortisol) response—the body stores fat and burns protein instead. It's like using kindling wood to keep the stove hot.

Cortisol is designed to signal the body to relax and refuel after periods of stress. So back in our primitive caveman days, cortisol's job was to keep us away from the sabre-tooth tigers and the other numerous dangers we faced.

Today we have this stress response all day long. Cortisol is released while we're on the road, at work and at home watching CSI. We often have overweight patients who say, "I don't eat all day, but when I get home, all I want to do is sit on the couch and eat. We call this couch potato syndrome. All day long they keep going, getting busier and busier and by the end of the day cortisol is screaming to the body, "Relax and refuel!" This is why people arrive home feeling tired, lethargic and hungry.

So we tell our clients that stress can be more fattening than chocolate. We've all heard people say they just have to look at chocolate and gain weight. Maybe it's the stress of not having the chocolate that is triggering the weight gain? After all, of the top ten life stressors, dieting is ranked seventh!

Brain-Based Solutions

We're now going to go over some of the brain-based solutions that can help the body deal with stress. The first thing that can help is to do a deep breathing exercise; we want to be exhaling twice as long as we inhale. So we breathe in to the count of four, and breathe out to the count of eight.

During the exhalation we stimulate the parasympathetic system and during inhalation we stimulate the sympathetic system. We want to be stimulating the parasympathetic system twice as long to help us achieve the relaxation response.

Other simple things that can help are taking a nice relaxing walk, being in nature, having a belly laugh, and having love in our lives. All of these are easy, natural ways that dissipate stress and neutralize it. But we also have the ability to use and practice Brain-Based Wellness to automatically override your thinking, anxiety and your stress, allowing the body to go into the relaxation response, and to reverse the effects of the fight-or-flight response.

We have been very successful in marketing weight loss in our clinics, along with hundreds of other doctors. By marrying brain-based solutions with a natural and healthy weight loss nutritional system, we are making the mind/body connection it takes to get permanent success.

One of the things we do at our clinic is hold a seminar called "How Stress is Making You Fat." We advertise this when we're on a radio show or a talk show in the area; we also put it in our active client base so they can bring their family and friends along.

In fact some of the things we've been discussing within this book are also discussed with our clients during the seminar. It's designed to be fun, engaging and easy to do. The idea is to get them to come in to the clinic and try out the brain-based solution so they can have a positive response and start to get results.

In our office we have a classroom model as well. This is not the only model you can have, but it is one way of providing patients the support they need. Later on in this chapter we're going to be hearing from Dr. Todd Singleton, a chiropractor who has put together a nutrition-based weight loss protocol that simply can't be beat. He will be sharing his seminar model with you as well.

Seminars are a great tool for you to utilize because it takes out some of the work involved. By holding a seminar you can see many people at once and figure out who is interested and who isn't.

We use flyers, posters, direct mail, email and traditional advertising to fill our seminars. It really doesn't take a lot of effort to get out there and start promoting the seminars. You can start with your existing patient base. We'll also provide you a link where we have Dr. Cynthia Porter presenting the class, so you get an idea of how she presents one of her seminars from start to finish.

Now we've also got people in our clinic who can do the seminar for us. It doesn't have to be the doctor. You can have your salesperson do the seminar, for example, because it's all PowerPoint driven. All the information you need is already there, someone who is well spoken and comfortable in front of group just needs to present it.

One of the reasons some doctors struggle with doing the presentation side of the seminar is because they are under stress themselves. They need to be using the brain-based solution to get into the relaxation response. The shift out of beta mode and into theta and alpha on a regular basis will rebalance their brains.

In our clinics we see people in groups of 12-25 at a time. Let's give you a little visual here. We have 12 recliners, a TV to show the

PowerPoint and a presenter standing at the front and presenting the class. We call this the "Classroom model."

There are several benefits to working the classroom model. First and foremost, you're giving more value, so you get higher fees. Moreover, everyone is coming in at once so you only need to do one session instead of twelve.

In most chiropractic offices, if the doctor doesn't have their hands on somebody, they're not making money. In this case you can have up to 25 people in front of you taking the class at once.

Now it's more value because it's an easier sale. Patients want support even if they don't admit it out loud, or even to themselves.

We have 26 specific classes that are geared to our supplement program called Solutions4. Whatever your philosophy is for nutrition, this is where you're going to educate your patients in groups. We think it's beneficial for the doctor to be doing the seminars because it helps to build stronger bonds. We like to do it when possible because we get the chance to interact with our patients, and they get to know us. Again the benefit is we don't have to see everyone one-at-a-time, which in a clinic would take an hour each instead of a chiropractic adjustment that might take a few minutes.

Another benefit of the seminar is it gives you the opportunity to sell the recommended products and supplements. We tell our staff that when they're up there talking about a product, hold it in your hand, and show it to them. If they follow those recommendations, just by talking about a product you have in your hand, making it on special at the clinic at the time, you're going to sell a lot of supplements. We sell close to $10,000 worth of supplements every week in our California clinic and it's mostly done through the classroom model.

Another thing we do is take the opportunity to up-sell the seminars to our chiropractic patients. In our classrooms, if we have empty chairs, we invite our active chiropractic patients to bring in family and friends to take up those other chairs. It also gives you a chance to tell them about all the other things you offer in your clinic and it keeps them engaged.

Now the way we've designed these seminars is we have a 20-minute class followed by a 20-minute SMT session that's the Brain-Based Wellness component.

Classes create energy and excitement in the clinic. When you have your group of patients, even five to ten, the energy level in the clinic is going to be so much different than just one patient coming in at a time. So it makes a big difference to provide patients ongoing knowledge, support and success strategies.

Keep in mind, too, that you have a captive audience. As mentioned, we have a television at the front of the room where we show slides designed to give the high points, which we play on an auto-loop while they're waiting for the class to start.

Also when we have successful clients in the room, we like to utilize them by getting them to step up and talk about their success. These heartfelt testimonials help the other people in the room to stay encouraged and motivated to get the results they want. Like anything, there are limitations to the classroom model. It obviously requires physical space and there are a lot of doctors out there who won't have the space to be able to deliver the classroom model; it just won't work in smaller spaces.

When we talk about space, our office in California is 4,000 square feet. Dr. Singleton's office is about 6,000 square feet. It's one of the biggest offices I have ever seen. But neither of us started there. We started where we were and grew. So of course when we're talking about the classroom model, it's important we focus on the key benefits, but we're not telling you to run out and get more office space; start off with what you have and build up from there.

Take-Home method

The take-home method is best for people who have smaller

offices. I always use as an example a doctor who has an exceptionally small clinic. You will see a zero-gravity chair in the corner of his room where he has his patients do demos. He has an open bay office, so he doesn't have an extra room available. He has people listen and then he sells them a take-home program. He doesn't have a set-up for his patients within his clinic, so he includes the MindFit Neuro-Trainer in his program price, provides them the appropriate sessions, and the patients listen from home.

It's very easy to implement the take-home method, which means we give our clients the equipment, we show them how to use it, we give them the proper supplementation and we give them the reading material. It doesn't require any additional space, so you could do this in a 400 to 600 square foot space, if that's what you have. We have some doctors who buy the MindFit and ask us to drop ship it to their patients, so there can be little to no expense in setting this up.

As with everything, there are some limitations to the take-home method. First, it requires a little more one-on-one time. Remember, you're going to have to sit down with each individual client and explain how the MindFit works. What we do with the take-home model in our own clinics is every week we call them on the telephone and we do a coaching session to make sure everything is working as it should. Also, in our offices, we use Dr. Todd Singleton's method for the physical side, so we have them come in once a month for a body wrap.

While the take-home method means that the patients are doing a little more on their own, if administered properly, they can still get excellent results. We make a staff member responsible for the patient to make sure they go through the whole program.

The other thing is you obviously have fewer opportunities to sell them additional products because they are not coming into your office a couple of times a week. They might go to a local pharmacy or a big box store where they're going to get inferior supplementation. There are plenty of brands out there, but you obviously want to make sure they are getting a good brand.

You will also have fewer opportunities to upsell chiropractic. So what we would recommend for those of you opting for the take-home method is you link them to some kind of chiropractic care. You can have them come in and do their adjustment and then do the coaching session at the same time.

Enrolling

Before you can enroll any patients in your programs, you must first enroll your staff. We don't want you to limit your time as the doctor. In fact, the doctor should not be implementing this program. You should be "prescribing" the brain-based solution as part of the patient's program, and the staff should be doing the rest.

For this reason, we recommend you set aside some time for your staff to do SMT sessions. In our office we have regular breaks and we have wellness breaks. So we have our staff experience SMT during the day so they get the recharge they need to stay upbeat and positive throughout their shift. It's important to have meetings with your staff about what you're doing so you understand and your staff understands what you want and need as the doctor so you can focus on getting the results for the patients; you need to set goals.

Choose a staff member to champion the program, then work together to go over the benefits of Brain-Based Wellness and gather together ideas for when and where patients can try it.

Think about your own office and all of the different ways you can implement this. Decide on an action plan, start using it and start using this in your practice. The key to this is implementation. When you enroll in our location license program, we're going to give you an e-copy of Dr. Todd's book so you can truly see for yourself he is a weight loss expert and you will also learn how he has integrated the brain-based wellness solution perfectly into his program. We want you to establish yourself as the weight loss expert in your home town.

First, you're going to open the conversation with the clients who need it the most. We're also going to give you a sheet we use in

our clinic to make people aware of the benefits of brain-based wellness
for weight loss. We're going to give you an introductory letter you can
give to them to make them aware of the services you're offering in your
clinic.

We're also going to provide you with the press release that
announces your new services. You will be able to modify it for your
own purposes; this is extremely important, you need to start using the
"How Stress Affects Weight Loss" in your clinic as quickly as possible.
This has all been thoroughly tried and tested and shown to be extremely
effective.

When we talk about enrolling, we're talking about engaging
people. This is the sales strategy we're going to teach you and it's a
lot like when you're doing a report of findings. There are some very
good people in the chiropractic world and when you think about their
manner and the way they engage, that's the first step. You should never
interrupt somebody's pain; you need to let them speak about it. You
need to be able to understand them and that's one of the things Dr.
Covey says in his groundbreaking book, The Seven Habits of Highly
Effective People, that to be understood you have to listen. Once you
start to listen, you can begin to understand where they are coming
from, so you can resolve their concerns and offer solutions to their
problems. You want to be able to open their minds to the possibility
that the things they have been doing up to this point haven't worked
for a reason, and that's why they came to you. Your job is to help them
realize that they need to be doing something different, and when they
follow a system that has been proven to work in the past, it will work
for them, too!

This is when we lead them and test them. We let them try out
the equipment for themselves. We let them try the demo session so
they experience it, and see what it can do for them; the system itself
will sell the program for you, you just need to leverage them a little.
Here is what we find is the hardest thing for doctors: They don't know
how to ask somebody for money. You've got to use your leverage, which
means you need to get the patient's criteria to be able to leverage them
into the right program. In later chapters we're going to spend a lot of

time talking about how to sell the program and how to enroll your patients. But we want you to understand there is a system in place where you can learn how to do what other people seem to be able to do naturally.

When we met Dr Todd Singleton a few years ago, we were blown away by the fantastic results he was getting in weight loss. We talked about how to integrate a program for Brain-Based Wellness and we called it "Overcoming Emotional Eating." Dr. Todd has been kind enough to share some advice to help you understand what it takes if you want to go out full force with a weight loss program. There are no other systems we know of that utilize this kind of powerhouse combination of Brain-Based Wellness, nutritional know-how, and top-shelf supplementation, that has been proven to work.

Club Reduce
By Dr. Todd Singleton

Over the last four years we've trained about 530 clinics in our weight loss protocols. Every month we offer a weekend training in our office. Years ago, after working with hundreds of weight loss patients, we recognized the need for an emotional eating component to our program, but there was very little available.

At first, we used Emotional Freedom Training (EFT) in an effort to help our patients overcome the emotional component of their weight problem. While we were seeing some results with EFT, it required a lot of a one-on-one time with the patient, and some of them found it a bit funky and confusing.

We heard about Dr. Porter's brain-based system from other chiropractors who had integrated his system in their practices and had become raving fans. We decided we needed to find out more.

Once we saw and experienced for ourselves what Dr. Porter was doing, we knew this was a missing link we needed to add to our weight loss programs so people would not have to white-knuckle it. They could be relaxed, positive and inspired, and be successful.

I'd also had my own personal experience with Dr. Porter's program. I used to regularly go over to this place to get a bean burrito with jalapeños; they were amazing tasting and it had become almost a daily habit. I started to listen to Dr. Porter's SMT and without even realizing it, I had stopped going over there. Then one day I decided to stop by and order that same bean burrito with these jalapeños and it didn't even taste the same. Dr. Porter's program totally got me away from eating the foods that are bad for you. So I know first-hand this program works and I wasn't even trying to make it work. I was listening to it and it worked.

Now we have our doctors coaching patients using SMT because a lot of patients want to lose weight but they've tried and failed at all of the other programs out there. They want to lose weight so badly, but for whatever reason, they keep falling into the same old traps. They'll say, "I don't know, I failed at so many other programs, I don't know if I can do this."

Now, one of our closing techniques is to have them come in and listen to some of the SMT, which we call the BBW protocol. Basically it's positive affirmations to help the patient realize they can do this and be successful. After about two to three sessions, we meet with them again and the close is a lot easier. They realize that their thoughts led them to the body they have and by changing your thoughts you can change your body.

We developed the Club Reduce program because we know that chiropractors are busy with their practice, so we developed a program you can literally turn over to your staff and you can leave them to the day-to-day running of it. Right now my staff generates between $125,000 to $150,000 a month just with the weight loss program.

Everyone has those moments where they look at the magazines and they say, "I want that body, that's what I want to be like." Intuitively they're thinking, "I want to be better, I should be like a thin person." For example, when they see somebody eating a salad in a restaurant and they think, "That's how I should be eating," but then they talk themselves out of it. "Well maybe I'll start Monday, all diets start on a Monday."

We get them in our office doing a body wrap or something and we have them listening to the brain-based experience to change their perception of what they think happiness is as far as food, and bring them to a more positive affirmation, thinking, "I can do this."
Our staff has already listened to SMT regularly so they know it, they love it and they're sold on it and the benefits it brings. They're always looking for ways to further incorporate it into our practice and bring it to the clients.

My staff will sometimes come to me and say something like, "Brenda's here. She's having problems with insomnia." Well if she's on our weight loss program, she's already experienced Dr. Porter's system. So we'll have her listen to the insomnia program, it will not only help her insomnia, but it will help with her weight loss as well, because we know you have to sleep so many hours a night in order for weight loss to be successful.

Great, now tell us how you implemented BBW to make your office more profitable? Well when they first come in we explain to them about how our clinic is different because we offer them the programs for getting healthy, not just losing weight. Every program has books, has menu plans, and recipes so they are able to start getting the whole family healthier, incorporating healthy living into their children's lives so they start getting better grades at school. Families start having better relationships and we see better libido (male and female) across the board. So there are lots of added benefits on top of weight loss when you start thinking and eating healthier.

As we're telling them this we're letting them know these are the sorts of results they can be achieving for themselves. As I said earlier, we have them test it out like a test drive when you buy a car; we let them test drive it and everybody loves it.

Everybody loves how they feel right after because twenty minutes of this is the equivalent of having a three-hour nap; it's when you tell your patients this they realize this program is so different from other programs out there and it's easier to sell the programs because

we're offering this new technology they've not had access to before.
The whole basis of this program that other programs don't have is we're
working on changing the brain so we can change the body. This is
something other programs don't do and this is why you're going to be
successful in our program where you haven't been before.
Can you tell the doctors some of the different ways you utilize it? You've
already mentioned a few, but how many of the different ways do you
use in your clinic?

When patients come in we help coach them. We have them
use the system when they're undergoing some of the other therapies
we offer such as the body wraps. We customize our treatments to suit
our individual patients depending on what program they're on. So our
customers get the feeling the program is customized to them and their
individual needs.

One thing we've noticed is your office is continuing to grow;
do you think there's any shortage of people in need of weight loss? Do
you think there are enough weight loss clinics out there for everybody?
You have to realize that 60 to 80 percent of the population is looking
for a weight loss solution at any one time. We have one doctor in
Illinois who averages around $4,000 to $6,000 a month from a town
of 150 people. So there are definitely people out there looking for this
kind of program and as we said this is something you can have your
staff implement so you can have a hands-off approach as a sideline
project to your chiropractic clinic. You can know people are going to
go somewhere to get this done, and it can be extremely profitable very
quickly. Literally within two weeks of starting with the program, we've
had doctors earning between $15,000 and $30,000. It's very easy and
quick to implement this as well; we have marketing as low as $200 a
month.

You don't have to go out there and get any new office space
either, we have doctors using the space for chiropractic from say 9-12
and then again between 3-6; you can now use the same space for your
weight loss program between 12-3 and 6-8. So it's entirely viable for
you to have staff there running the weight loss program. I leave at 5
o'clock and we're open until 8.

Of the average patient that comes to one of your 500 weight loss clinics what percentage of them succeed at losing their weight?

One hundred percent of them succeed if they do the program; that's what's so cool about this. I tell the patient, "I can guarantee the program, but I can't guarantee that you're going to do it." So that's where we're going to hold their hand, we're going to call them once a week and we're going to see them in the clinic once a week. I've had doctors call me up and say, "I had a patient who lost 22 pounds and she's plateaued for the last three weeks."

I say to them, "Have you gone over her booklet, are you going over her menu plan?" They have to eat enough calories so we give them a booklet on nutrition because this is not a starvation diet. The answer I get is usually, "Oh no, I haven't been looking at their book." So there's always a reason why things might not be working, but if the patient is doing it right, it works 100 percent of the time.

For the average patient you have coming in to one of your weight loss clinics, how much weight are they typically losing on average?

That's a good question but it depends on obviously how overweight the patient is to start with. We have one lady who came in and she lost eight inches with one of our body wraps in one visit. But patients can lose anywhere between give to over 125 pounds; but usually the average is around 10 to 15 pounds a month based on the results we've seen in our clinics, that's a healthy one to three pounds per week.

Again for the average patient you have coming into your office, how long are they in your office doing the weight loss program. Is it a 30-day, 60-day, 90-day cycle or longer?

We have different programs according to what we think our individual patients need. I have developed a system where the patient fills out a form, and the doctor and the staff then review it. Based on the results and what the patient has said, they can go into the 20-day,

5-week, 2-month, 3-month or 6-month program. Our main program is a 3-month program, that's $2000 for 3 months. Then we have the maintenance program. Around 90 percent of people go into the maintenance program, which we sell for $500 or $1,500; that's for a year-long program.

With Dr Porters system, the Self-Mastery Technology, you don't sell on a per visit basis do you, you sell as part of the package, is that right?

Yes, that's correct. After the 3-months of weekly visits we sell the patient the 1-year maintenance program. Then according to the package they buy, either the $500 or the $1,500, we sell them one of Dr. Porter's systems for home care. We never sell the light-and-sound technology upfront unless it is a take-home program due to distance or travel issues. After they've gone through the program, the MindFit becomes part of their home care program.

Do you have any parting comments before we finish?

As chiropractors, we should continue adjusting the spine. In fact, many of our doctors who are offering the weight-loss program are also adjusting patients as part of the program, and they're calling it a weight-loss adjustment.

I think one Club Reduce doctor in Oklahoma said it best: "This system is amazing because adding weight loss has doubled my chiropractic practice. People are coming in now who weren't coming to see me as a chiropractor. They now have trust and confidence in me." So this is a great way to build your chiropractic practice as well.

To learn more about Dr. Singleton's Club Reduce program, visit doctorsgoldmine.com

Assignment

So in this chapter we want you to go over again how stress affects weight loss. Role-play a weight loss evaluation with your family members and your staff members so you can start to ask the right questions. When you're asking questions, you're now in control and you're also listening to them for feedback.

Set a date to send out your first press release; press releases are free. The rule of thumb is that you need to put out at least 10 percent in marketing for what you want to make back in sales, but anything you can get for free is a bonus.

Research any additional steps you might need to take to start successful and probable weight loss programs.

We hope you will take the time to go through this more than once, get comfortable with it, open up your mind, open up your heart, start implementing these ideas, these services, expand your practice, expand your outreach and expand your clinical results.

Get out of your comfort zone. Get comfortable being uncomfortable. That's where all the growth lies. Make sure you continue to connect and enroll and engage with all these modules.

Let's keep growing together, and let's keep changing the world to become a better and healthier place.

CHAPTER

SIX

**The most effective way to incorporate
Brain Based Wellness into a
Chiropractic Practice.**

The most effective way to incorporate
Brain Based Wellness into a Chiropractic Practice

This module, as the title suggests, is going to focus on the most effective ways for you to incorporate Brain-Based Wellness into your existing chiropractic practice. Hopefully by now you've got your mind-set right. We've been through the planning stages and now we're ready to start putting things into action.

So, how do we incorporate this into the chiropractic practice? The critical question we should be asking is: Why do we want to incorporate Brain-Based Wellness into a chiropractic practice?

We talked about this briefly in previous chapters, but the main points are we want to have quicker, better and more sustainable clinical outcomes and results. We want to do the best thing for our patients, and get the best clinical results. Of course, we also want to enhance our own reputation in the process. We understand our clinical outcomes have a direct effect on our personal incomes.

The second reason is it helps to increase our ability to attract new patients to the practice. For example, we can now market ourselves as a natural weight loss clinic, insomnia clinic, or stress reduction clinic, in addition to being a chiropractic clinic. It increases our patient base and improves our compliance by getting better results for our patients.

Our doctors are consistently growing their PVA, their retention and their compliance. The final result we're all ultimately working towards is greater profitability. We all want to help our patients get better clinical results and generate greater profitability as a result of that, almost as a side-effect.

Incorporating BBW
as a non-insurance dependent profit center

Our basic philosophy is to create a practice that is not insurance dependent. We are not against insurance nor are we advocating an all cash practice. However, we want to train our patients to value their

care and to realize that paying for care is their responsibility. The goal
is to have each patient view their care in your office as a necessity and
not as a luxury.

The reality is weight loss isn't being covered by insurance anyway. However, now that the AMA has classified obesity as a disease,
this may soon change. So weight loss is something your patients are
going to pay cash for; they're going to pay it to somebody, whether it
is membership at Weight Watchers at $20-$25 a week or they're going
to pay you for your program to achieve weight loss through a healthy
mind and body.

The same can be said for stop smoking. Even though we've
gone from 55 percent of the population being smokers 20 years ago to
19 percent today, there's still a large pool of people willing and wanting
to pay cash for this service.

Just as a comparison, the patch was such an ineffective method
of helping people quit smoking they took it off prescription. It's now
sold over-the-counter if you want to use it, but statistically, it's not even
as good as the placebo. The placebo is 33 percent effective, but the
patch is even lower than that.

People who smoke are already spending conservatively between
100-$200 a month on their habit. As chiropractors we're hoping to
shift into a more wellness-based practice where people are willing to
pay out of their own pockets.

Out-of-pocket health expenditures have tripled in the last five
years. So we have people wanting to stay pain free and they're learning
they can do it through Brain-Based Wellness and it supports the chiropractic solution.

Stress reduction is where this technology really focuses. When
the brain waves are out of balance, the patient is operating in high beta
and not able to get into the alpha and theta brain wave patterns that
generate creativity and relaxation. When they are not able to get those
in synch with their lifestyle then the body is out of balance from the

brain to the body, or the body to the brain; however you want to think about it. We are going to be the mind side of health by getting people to think differently about what's happening in their lives so they can handle it without the repercussions of discomfort in the body caused by stress.

Of course another of the problems we have a program for is insomnia. Statistics say one out of six adults have some form of insomnia, which means they're not sleeping through the night. They are not getting into the delta rhythm of sleep they need to recharge and rejuvenate. We've seen nothing but positive benefit with Brain-Based Wellness in relation to insomnia. We've sold well over a hundred thousand units since the 1980s, and better sleep is consistently a side-benefit people see.

The statistics for insomnia over age 50 are much worse than in other demographics, making it another growing market of people in search of a natural solution. If you have patients who are having problems with insomnia, this technology will get the results they are looking for and they will start to sleep within one to five weeks of using the technology—and some people see results virtually overnight.

People are willing to pay for brain-based treatments because they want to get out of pain. One of the great things about Brain-Based Wellness is people will start to see results almost immediately, even with the 10-minute demonstration we provide. And so far we've named just some of what we offer for which people will be willing to pay out of pocket to get results.

As a practicing chiropractor, just stop and think about what percentage of your patient base is overweight or obese or just want to lose a bit of weight? How many of your patients are stressed out? What percentage of your patient base suffers from chronic pain? How many want (or need) to stop smoking? How many can't fall asleep or wake up multiple times through the night?

You can start to get a sense of the number of patients you have coming through your office who could benefit from Brain-based Wellness. Again, we shouldn't lose sight of the fact that this also widens the net in our marketing. There are literally thousands, if not tens of thousands of people in your community suffering from these problems who have no idea that you have the solution. Unfortunately, we still live in a world where people in your community might come to see you for these issues, but still might resist going to the chiropractor for chiropractic problems. However, once they know and trust you, the likelihood of their becoming lifelong patients increases dramatically.

Doctors are already getting results

In 2006 we did a weight loss study with Dr Scott Newman from California. When we originally asked him to put this technology into his clinic, his response was, "Well, where's your study?"

There have, in fact, been quite a few studies proving this technology, but we felt it would be helpful to do some of our own studies, especially in the weight loss arena. With Dr Newman, we did our own 12-week weight loss study. We didn't give them the nutrition classes, which are available to any doctor who buys the Brain-Based Wellness location license, but we wanted to keep it simple. So patients just listened to the sessions that we call our Emotional Eating Series.

Over the course of 12 weeks, the average participant lost over a pound a week, without any other instruction. We didn't give them any coaching sessions, we didn't tell them what to eat or not eat; we just had them come in during their chiropractic care and listen to a session. That convinced Dr Newman to implement Brain-Based Wellness into his own practice long term.

We did another study in Texas with a mixed medical group of doctors that included chiropractors as well as medical doctors, called American Pain and Wellness; they asked if they could do a pain study. The current MindFit system we use is based on technology originally designed in the 80s for pain clinics. This technology works for pain because when you are in a state of alpha and theta, you feel no pain. Pain is only registered in the body when you are in beta. So if you greatly reduce beta waves, the patient feels little or no pain or discomfort in the body. This is why certain people have what we refer to as a high pain threshold. Really what they have is a lot of alpha and theta waves and they are able to diminish or reduce their beta waves.

The study by American Pain and Wellness was comprised of 30 patients who had suffered botched surgeries. They'd all had surgeries where some nerve damage had occurred that caused intense pain for which no amount of medication could help.

This was another 12-week study. During the study, they found that over 80 percent of the patients were pain free after the third week. However, they had the patients continue listening to the program to cement the changes in their brains and ensure the pain would not return.

Half of the patients were able to remain pain free between each session. Ultimately, nearly all were able to manage their own pain at home just by using the equipment, with no medication or anything else.

Now just as a side-note, you may be wondering about side effects. The great answer to that question is there are no side-effects. Your patients are going to be able to sleep better, reduce stress and lose weight and there are going to be no nasty side effects to deal with, and especially not the kind associated with medications—such as sluggishness and addiction.

However, that's not strictly true. There was one unexpected side effect discovered during the pain study, but it was a good one. One day one of the researchers called and asked, "What suggestions did you give our patients for weight loss in the program when they're listening?" The answer was, "We didn't give them any weight loss suggestions in the pain series."

"Well, something happened," he said, "Because the average weight loss was just under a pound a week for the patients participating in the pain study."

That was great news, and not a total surprise. You see, when cortisol levels are returned to normal and innate intelligence is able to bring the body back to homeostasis, the body goes to work dealing with the key issues that were ignored for so long. This means the program not only worked to reduce their pain but it also helped them lose weight.

Another example of a doctor using the equipment and getting results is Dr Shelly Dowling of Denver, Colorado. When she consistently started ordering 10 to 20 MindFit units at a time for reselling in her clinic, we had to ask her what was going on because she was achieving above average results for a very small office—typically our doctors will sell around 5 to 10 units a month.

She said that she started off in only a 200-square foot office and thus didn't have the room in her clinic to run the program, so she decided to do a bit of a study of her own. She started sending her patients home with MindFit units and soon discovered that those patients using the system at home got well over a 50 percent increase in the results they were previously getting with their weight loss program on its own. So this links back to what we were saying in one of the previous chapters, you need to stop and think about how best to work the program for you and the facilities you have. She thought about whether she should get a bigger space; but in the end the best way to implement the program for her was to allow the patients to use the equipment at home and to do her coaching over the phone.

She also runs a detoxifying cleanse program, so her patients purchase the cleanse supplements and MindFit and they go home and use it. She was already coaching them and tracking their results, and she soon realized that they were getting much better results by using the MindFit from home. It makes sense, if you're doing SMT at home every day, or even every other day, you're going to get better results than if you're just using it twice a week like they do when they come in the clinic for the program.

Do the results last?

It's all very well talking about the great results people get when they first start using SMT, but whether these results are sustainable is the real issue and the thing most of you are probably wondering.

No question, Dr. Singleton and the Club Reduce doctors were already getting great weight loss results before they integrated SMT into their program. However, the challenge they were encountering involved patients' emotional eating, stress eating, and habitual eating. Consequently, some of their patients were not maintaining this weight loss after they finished the program. This is something they found greatly improved when they started integrating Brain-Based wellness. Patients were now getting great results, and they were also more successful at maintaining those results after the program ended.

So what we're talking about here is not only quick results, because most doctors know how to get their clients cleansed and get their body functioning well, but we are talking about the long-term results. That's what we really need to be aiming for, the long-term results that get people thinking like naturally thin people.

In addition to the success we're seeing as far as clinical results, we're also finding that clinics on average, when they get three or four months into implementing the program, especially the classroom model, and they follow the protocols, they can earn well over $100,000 a month, just by implementing Brain-Based Wellness. We've discussed this before but we're just going to go a further into how much space you need to implement the program.

How much space do I really need?

First of all, you already have an operational clinic, and there may be more space available there than you think, so we're not telling you to go out and rent new space. You can use a comfortable chair, a massage table, or your adjusting table; you can use the space you have right now and even put comfortable zero gravity chairs in your lobby or reception room.

Some doctors like to set up an SMT room, which is what we've done in our clinic. We have three recliners in our SMT room and we have three systems set up there. Many doctors have an extra office they're using as a storage room. With a little organization, that room can easily be converted to an SMT room.

When we talk about the classroom setting, we have one doctor who replaced the chairs in his lobby with recliners so when they are not seeing patients for chiropractic care they do their classes out in the lobby with the recliners. So if you don't have a spare room, you can set up your classroom in your lobby.

Be resourceful. If you have a room that's 15 x 10 then you can set up this classroom model, we do ours in a room that's 24 x 24. Again it depends on what way you want to go with this and what way you think will work the best for you, we just want to make you aware of all the possibilities and that space need not be a limiting factor.

So, you need the comfortable chair, a recliner, a massage table or an adjusting table. You need the MindFit Neuro-Trainer light and Sound system and an MP3 player. Of course, when you purchase one of the iPod Location License programs, you won't have to worry about that.

We've had a lot of great feedback from the doctors who have already used the program on how they are implementing it in their clinics without spending a lot of money. Many of them start with zero-gravity chairs that cost less than $100, are comfortable, and recline fully. You don't want a chair that only sits straight up and down as patients will have a hard time fully relaxing in this position.

A good percentage of patients will fall into a light asleep during their session, and of course you want them to be leaning backwards not forwards should they fall asleep.

So relative to the chair, having recliners is ideal. But if you're going to put multiple chairs in, or you don't have a lot of room or finances, zero-gravity chairs that you can purchase from a patio shop or online at Amazon.com or Walmart.com is a good secondary option. Of course if you have room for a massage table or chiropractic table that's great as well.

Headphones are another item you're going to need. You want to have over-the-ear headphones so you can clean them to ensure it's hygienic for each patient to use. You also need to have a volume control on them so when you leave the room the patient isn't stuck with the volume too low or too high. They need to be able to control it themselves. Again this doesn't have to be a big expenditure, you don't necessarily have to buy Bose headphones. You're looking for headphones with a decent quality because you want them to last, but they don't have to be the highest quality because that's not going to affect the process.

You should expect to pay no more than $49 for headphones that work great. No matter what you pay for headphones, the patient will have the same experience with the neurosensory algorithms.

So what we're trying to get at here is you need minimum space and you don't have to spend a lot of money to get started with the program; this immediately turns into a great system that helps your patients dramatically, allows you to attract more new patients into the clinic, improves your clinical results and generates a ridiculous amount of profit.

How much money will I need to invest initially?

There is a small investment to set up the program but the nice thing about the Brain-Based Wellness program is once you have it set up in your clinic, there are really no other expenses. It's not like a franchise where you have to pay a percentage of your sales back to someone. You can use your current staff.

Offering these services doesn't take a lot of staff time either. As long at the doctor is willing to have a conversation about Brain-Based Wellness with the patient, make the recommendation to the patient, and then have that patient do demo session with them, it's going to be very easy and low cost.

Implementing the program

We're going to give you the step-by-step process on how to implement this in your own practice. We're going to give you the marketing materials on how to go out and market this for your practice, how to communicate this to new and current patients, how to generate people to step-up and utilize a program of 12 weeks in stress management, or weight loss, and how to make it immediately effective and profitable. Now you may think we're going on about this a bit but the reality is some of the doctors who have already started to implement this are getting hung up one the incidentals and worrying about things they really don't need to be worrying about.

They're saying things like, "I'm not sure where to put this, I'm not sure I have enough room, I'm not sure I want to do this in my reception room, I have a closet, but I'd have to clear it out." We don't want to call them excuses, but they're finding all of these reasons why they can't implement the program right away and it's slowing them down and holding them back.

None of this is necessary. All you need is a place for the patient to sit or lie down comfortably and you need to tell them you're recommending this program as part of their care. During their case history, they may have told you they're stressed at home or work, they're overweight or whatever the topic is. Now you can tell them you have a way to help them. You tell them they need to get adjusted a specific number of times a week for a specific number of weeks, and then they're going to do this program for 12-weeks.

The doctors who are keeping this simple and basic are doing amazing with it. Some of them are seeing 20 or 30 patients a day or more after only having been running the program for 30 days.
We're bringing this up because we don't want those of you thinking about taking up the program to be put off by over-analyzing it, overthinking it, or trying to make it perfect; it's already perfect on its own. Just follow what we're teaching you, follow the sequence and start implementing. You'll be astonished by the outstanding results.

Managing the program

Let's talk about the management of the system once you have it implemented. We make it easy for any member of staff to run the program; in the insomnia program for example the MP3's are labeled as IR01 to IR05, this 1-5 refers to the week number. So as they are coming through the program, you just need to document the week they are on so they go through all of the programs in the correct order. One of the things we have found with Brain-Based Wellness and the neurosensory algorithms is your patients need a variety of exposures to the to get their brain in balance. Even though they may like one session better than others, they need to go through the whole series.

Someone asked us once why we have over 500 different sessions? The answer is because we need a series of different ways to look at the same problem. Think of it like cross training for the brain, we need to exercise it in many different ways to get results and our program specifically tracks this progress.

We typically recommend you do the adjustment first and have patients listen to the Brain-Based Wellness afterwards. This allows time to let their nervous systems adjust, and we find the more relaxed they are to start with, the better the program works.

Of course the order you do this in is up to you. Some doctors prefer to have their patients listen to the program and then do the adjustment afterwards.

We ask them questions every time they come in to document their progress through the program. For example, number one, can you tell me your level of motivation to get the results you want? They then give us a number between two and eight and we provide them the information they need to help them accomplish their goal. If we find our patients drops below a six on the scale, we sit them down and have a personal coaching session with them. It takes anywhere from five to ten minutes and we can get them back on track. So it's a way of documenting their progress to make sure they get their results.

We've also developed a manual for your staff to use as a guide-
line. This might not work specifically for your clinic because as we've
said you can tailor the program to suit your own needs at your own
clinic. However, this manual for staff members informs them and edu-
cates them about the program and what their responsibilities are in
using the system.

We've also had doctors asking us what they should be charging
and again there is no right answer. This is up to the individual doctor
to decide, especially since market sizes and demographics vary. But as a
rule of thumb, whatever you're selling your adjustments for, you should
be charging the same price for the SMT session.

Now this doesn't mean you necessarily have to charge them the
same way you charge for adjustments. In other words, you don't have
to charge by the session.

We recommend selling these services as a program. For instance, with insomnia we recommend you sell packages as a five-week
program, which includes ten sessions they'll do in the clinic. Those ten
sessions are say $50 each, that's $500 if they pre-pay for the package;
maybe we're going to discount it to the $450.

We like to offer 10 percent off as a motivational discount. We
find it helps to add a little bit more incentive to buy the package. We've
found it's just as easy for us to sell our patients a series of programs than
it is for us to sell them one. It's also beneficial for us as the doctor to sell
as a package.

If we're trying to sell them an individual session each week, it's
going to take a lot more of the doctor's time. Once our patients are
finished with their program, if they want to re-do that program or do
one of the other programs, we offer them a 25 percent discount off of
any future programs they want to purchase.

We always urge our licensees to price test. Let's say you're going
to offer your 5-week program for $500, or $100 a week. In California,
we might charge $1000 for that program because our costs are higher

and people are accustomed to paying more. So it really depends on where you are in the marketplace.

You're price testing to find out whether people will pay cash for the program, and whether they will pay in advance. If more than 50 percent of the people that sign up for your program pay in advance, you're probably pricing it too low. In some of the bigger cities where your cost of doing business is higher, you don't want to be too low-priced that you're not making the money you need.

You'll also want to leave yourself some room for discounting if needed. For example, if your program is priced at $1000 and they can't afford it, you can always say, "I really think you need this, so why don't I give you a discount and we can do it for $800." Keep in mind, you can always go down in price but you can't go up.

Again, the amount of discount we offer depends on whether they're already a patient on the chiropractic side, or whether we had to spend money on marketing to bring them into the clinic. If they're already a patient, we'd probably sell a $1200 for $1000 for the first program. Then, if they were to sign up for subsequent programs, you can offer them a greater discount.

On the other hand, if we're bringing in new patients, we don't necessarily give them a discount. Instead, we might offer them a complimentary chiropractic evaluation so we can cross them over and turn them into a new patient as well. We find the conversion from SMT patient to chiropractic patient averages in the neighborhood of 75 to 80 percent.

Those doctors who are doing the best at this program are finding there is a great crossover between the two programs, and they're typically the ones doing a membership discount for their existing clients.

We also often tell patients about family discounts, and what you'll find is as long as you have space, you can fill it up like an airplane. We sometimes use what we call a "Ticket to Ride." We have our patients give these tickets to their family and friends so they can come into the clinic. We have them sit them in the room we have set up for our SMT and we give them a free seminar to educate them and an SMT session so they can have the experience. We then invite them to attend an evaluation.

Logistically, if you only have one SMT listening station set up in your practice, it's quite possible for you to schedule a patient every half hour, because the sessions are approximately 20 minutes. This allows ten minutes of leeway. You'll have five minutes to get them in the chair, briefly set expectations (for new patients), set them up with the headphones and glasses, select the right program. Then you'll have five minutes at the end to remove the equipment, clean the headphones and glasses, and bring the patient back to the front desk for whatever's next. Remember, you can be doing 30-minute sessions all day long, even through the lunch break, by properly varying your staff's schedule. So say you're in the office for ten hours, you can see 20 patients a day with just one chair or station and, of course, this number grows proportionally as you add more stations; it's a relatively quick and easy process.

Top 5 Brain-Based Wellness Programs

While we can't tell you how much to charge for your program due to the many variables involved, we can certainly provide you some guidelines. Here are a few recommendations.

Weight loss

We find that most doctors selling weight loss programs charge between $1000 and $3000 for a 12-week program. There are two variables to consider. First, is what your market can bear and, second, what else you can bundle into your package to add value.

For example, a number of the doctors we work with also offer Dr. Singleton's Club Reduce program for weight loss (and neuropathy). With Club Reduce, in addition to SMT, you are providing nutritional supplements, coaching, body wraps and more. Thus, these doctors regularly charge $3000 or more. At the end of the program, they also sell a maintenance package that includes a MindFit for home care.

Consider what else you might offer to add value to your program. Perhaps there is a nutritional supplement line you can offer or you may want to add in weight loss adjustments to help free up the nervous system. The more you provide, the more you can charge and the better results you will get.

Stop smoking

With the stop smoking program, doctors are typically charging between $800 and $1500. Most will also sell a MindFit at the end of the program. This is because smoking is a form of self-medicating, so they need a tool to deal with stress and other issues they might have.

We should also say that, depending on the price of the program, you should consider including supplementation to help the patient get rid of all of those tobacco-related toxins. We have a program where we include supplementation and another where we don't. It's up to the doctor whether they want to include supplementation or not, but it can double the price of the program if they do, and it will get the patient feeling healthier and stronger faster, which improves their likelihood of succeeding for life.

Stress reduction

We have stress reduction programs starting from as low as $700 and they go up to $1000. So again it depends on what you want to do and then again, at the end of the program you can sell them the MindFit for home care. Let's remember that the majority of patients are always under stress and therefore will always benefit from an ongoing program.

Reselling the MindFit Neuro-Trainer

For several of the programs we've talked about selling the unit to the patient at the end of their program so they can continue at home on their own. For the pricing of this, we buy the units at $200 and we sell them to the patient for $395; so you pretty much double your money.

In addition, we recommend you sit down in front of the website with the patient and recommend what additional programs they should purchase. Many doctors help the patient purchase as much as a $1000 worth of programs and you make a commission on this as well. Now if you were to purchase the unit in packs of five or ten, then the price can go down to as low as $150; so then of course you will more than double your profit when you resell them to your patients. Then if you have any of your patients go back to their login online and purchase any additional software, which is $30 per session, you will get a percentage back from the sale of that session. So you will continue to earn money when patients buy a $30 download without having any inventory.

Pain control

When we talk about the Pain Control program we find most doctors will combine that with chiropractic care. The cost of the program can be between $1000 to $3000 for that first package. Then of course while they are coming in to the clinic for that package we sell them a longer program or put them on a maintenance care program on the chiropractic side. But you can also sell them the take-home package.

Insomnia

The Insomnia program runs for 5 weeks and we have the program priced from as low as $600 up to $1000. We find most people with insomnia will go through the program at the clinic and then they will purchase the equipment to take home as well.

Pretty much everyone who walks in your door is going to need help assisting their bodies and brains in dealing with stress and getting some proper nutrition. A lot of the programs work in conjunction with the different things people need to do to really keep their bodies and minds in balance. When we're practicing Brain-Based Wellness, we are achieving what we call the relaxation response. We've talked about this before, but it bears repeating because our goal is to reverse the effects of the fight-or-flight response.

With this over-stressed, over-stimulated lifestyle we're all living, we have to learn to take some down time for ourselves if we are thrive. If we don't, we're going to end up like the frog in the pot from the psychology experiment—if it doesn't know you're turning up the heat, it's eventually going to die.

We would never jump into many of the situations we find ourselves in if we knew how stressful things we're going to get, but life just happens that way without us even realizing it.

When we get our physiology and our psychology to match, balance and align, we experience optimal health and peak performance.

A Case Study with Dr. Jared Leon

Jared Leon is a sensational chiropractor in Long Island, New York and he is a long-time member of The Master's Circle. He is a functional neurologist and he gets amazing results in his clinic. Jared also lives what we would all refer to as the chiropractic lifestyle. He exercises regularly, eats amazingly healthy and nutritious foods, takes supplementation, gets adjusted regularly and he's just one of the healthiest people you'll ever meet.

You're using Brain-Based Wellness for yourself and your family, and you're now incorporating it into your practice, could you tell us why? Why did this whole concept of Brain-Based Wellness with Light and Sound technology make so much sense to you, you immediately wanted to take action and start utilizing it?

Initially it all started in a seminar. Dr Porter was the guest speaker at a Lunch and Learn and I was really excited to hear the potential of what he was saying and how it could be beneficial to my family, my practice and me. So I just decided to go ahead and give it a go at home. At the time, I was in the process of building a new office. So I would use it almost every day, I'd say six out of seven days a week, sometimes twice a day. I was mostly using a lot of the creativity SMT sessions as well as those specifically for stress relief.

As I continued with the program, the most amazing thing started to happen. I was able to visualize in ways I never could have imagined before. I was seeing how to construct the new office, what the room layout would look like, how I wanted the colors and patterns, and how it would all work together. I then brought the technology to my children who were give and seven at the time. I had them use the Enlightened Children Series and the first thing my seven-year old said to me was he felt so relaxed; so we just continued to use it every day.

Once I had fully implemented the program for my family, I decided to create a Brain-Spa room in my practice. This was just a room with a nice comfy chair and a little table. I wanted to create a space so it was almost as if you were sitting at home with the technology. The program is still attracting more and more patients to my practice, and everyday I'm letting more and more patients try everything about it.

What kind of results have they started to experience?

It's been really fun and exciting so far. I've had a lot of patients fall asleep really quickly. It just shows how out of balance they really are. We just leave them and when their session is up we'll go in and gently wake them up, and they'll be amazed by how they feel. Straight away they're asking me when they can try it again.

Everyone has absolutely loved the technology so far and has felt substantially better and more relaxed. I ask them when they come back if they've been sleeping better after using the technology and every one of them has said yes. So we've had great results so far.

Have you tried implementing it with the pre-framing comments as outlined in this book?

I've been working on it. I've been slowly integrating it differently and trying to get my verbiage down. It's figuring out the best way to say it and change it to suit your needs and your practice; that's currently what I'm working on right now. I've been trying to get more and more people every day. So I've set myself a goal every day for the amount of new patients I want to get in to try the MindFit.

We suggested to Jared that he start by doing a demo or trial with the patient, and the he introduce it in a way that presells them based on the results they are getting from the demo, something like this:

"You are now at that point in care where I want to do a test to see if you will flourish with this amazing new technology in addition to your chiropractic care to help you live your best life. There are three possible results I am looking for that will show me it is a positive test. If you fall asleep, are centered balanced or relaxed...or if you feel totally focused, energized and reinvigorated...or if you temporarily feel a little woozy or lightheaded because your brain experienced both of the other two responses in such a short time, then I know this will help you flourish and thrive with care."

Can you tell us about how you're selling this in your office, how easy that has become, what kind of resistance, if any, you've been experiencing, and how you're implementing this as a profit-center?

We're still in the infancy stage, but when we first started to implement the program I chose two long-term patients, to try out the technology as a reward for their loyalty and respect over the years. I said, 'Let's try this brand new technology on you, and in return if you could just give me some feedback that would be great.'

So I then let them try it free for give sessions, but by the third session they were completely hooked and were asking where they could buy one for themselves. Initially I bought 5 units from Dr. Porter and I sold two of the units to my two trial patients. They then went home and started downloading the programs. So right away, just from those two trial patients, I literally made back all of my money just from sell-

ing them the technology and the sessions they bought. So right away I
was in the black, which is amazing for a product I had just bought and
just started to implement.

Have you encountered any resistance from any patients?

No, nobody has given me any resistance. The only thing I
would say is that in my last office I had my room set up using a chiropractic table; to them it wasn't as comfortable as it could have been. In
my new office I've created a space with a much nicer looking lounger
and it's just been great. That was really it, nobody has said anything
negative about the program itself; it's all been really positive.

Could you just give us an insight into some of the things you
are planning to implement from the Brain-Based Wellness system?

I can't wait to look at the protocol sheets because I think that is
something that would have really helped me when I first got started in
this process; but I know they will be able to give me some great insights
even now that I am already started.

I'm excited about the top five programs you have already outlined. I'm going to create something I can show to prospective patients
to advertise to them the top give programs we have for them to utilize.
They're so overwhelming in their popularity in my opinion, and everyone you know, family, friends, patients; they're all going to have at least
one of these problems. So once they see this, they start to ask questions
about the program and I can educate them about the problems they're
having and ways in which I can help them.

The other thing I am looking forward to is the CA manual,
I can't wait to read it and write down all the actual modules and the
order in which they were designed to be played. So far I have just been
letting my patients listen to the module they think will be most beneficial to them, so they've really had some leeway in what they listen
to. But I am really excited about the idea of having them go through
the program in a certain order, and the order they were designed to be
used.

I also can't wait to take the literature and create a slide show in my office. I've put a nice big screen in the office and I want to create a slide show about how powerful some of these different modules could be. With weight loss, for example, I think it's even more profound when you break it apart and look at the 52 sessions. Just hearing the titles Dr. Porter has created, I think that alone will inspire questioning.

It really got my brain working on how we can create new financial plans, adding it in as another bonus to my long-term wellness cases. It just gave me a lot of things to think about and it was a really great module.

Could you just spend a few seconds and speak about the connection between this Brain Based Wellness model with the Light and Sound Technology to what you do as a chiropractor, the congruency of the two things together?

I think nothing was cooler than seeing it live at the last seminar I attended in Orlando. They picked a random doctor out of the audience to utilize with NeuroInfiniti. To see the brain mapping was amazing to me to see the actual change to the highest level. To get optimally healthy you have to have a balanced brain. That's something I look at every single day in the practice. I can balance someone's brain, but am I balancing brain waves? The answer is I never thought of it that way before.

Now that I have this technology, I can utilize chiropractic as the ultimate driving force to optimize a person's nervous system by balancing the brain. How cool can it be to balance the actual brain waves and see that you're doing it? This to me is the most exciting thing I've had in years. I can connect the two together—chiropractic and Brain-Based Wellness—to have the perfect marriage and help my patients the best way I can. It's amazing and I think it's right in sync with chiropractic. It's everything we speak about just on a different level. In school we never talked about brain waves, so I thought it was dynamite that I could now explain pain as far as the different brain waves go. Now I tell my patients that with stress you're going to have increased pain because you have increased beta, but if we increase the alpha and theta then you're not going to be stressed and will have far less pain. It's profound.

What do you see as the next phase of this system in your practice?

As that system gets its own energy, it will just keep growing and growing. That's why I really think the slideshow is going to be one of the coolest things, and putting posters out there because the true benefits of the program are amazing. To know you can increase serotonin by an average of 21 percent within one session of 22 minutes, it's just amazing stuff."

Assignment

Let's get to this week's assignment. We want you to watch "How to set up a ZenFrames listening station" on YouTube (ZenFrames is the former name of the MindFit Neuro-Trainer.) Have your staff role play setting up the patients. Remember, we want to get a patient into the system every 30 minutes; how do we set it up, how do we organize it, how do we get them off, how to we clean the headphones, an so forth. You want to set the goal to have 75 percent of your patients do a free complimentary demo in the next 30 days. We would again suggest you try to pre-frame them and tell them in advance what they should be experiencing, and if they do experience those things, it's a positive test they will benefit from using the program

Then set a goal for what percentage of those people you are going to convert into selling a package. Ideally, we're looking for 100 percent.

Begin price testing with your patients, you have to come up with a number that's comfortable and reasonable. Start with the structure we gave you for pricing.

Most importantly, take time each day to use the technology yourself. Go to TMCO2, optimize it, optimize your practice, and start to experience it yourself. Get some experience with it and see for yourself the same things we've discovered, that Jared Leon discovered, and so many others—that this stuff is absolutely amazing and works great.

It's a matter of implementation, if you follow our guidelines, then you will start to see definite improvement. There's no fear here, just let the patients get on and they'll do the selling for you. That's the number one step.

Enjoy, keep growing, keep helping and serving your patients, and as a terrific side-effect, keep making a ridiculous amount of money.

CHAPTER
SEVEN

**What is the most effective way to
introduce it into your practice?**

What is the most effective way to introduce Brain-Based Wellness into your practice?

In this chapter we're going to be discussing the Brain-Based Wellness marketing system and discovering the most effective ways to introduce it into your practice.

Because we're not experts on everything, we've asked a true expert, Dr. Cynthia Porter, to take us through the advertising process. Cynthia was responsible for building our franchise company. We built our marketing system on the premise that you can have a good product, but if you don't have effective marketing for that product, it doesn't do you much good. So Cynthia has put together some important marketing training for you. We know a lot of people want to know why our marketing works when other marketing doesn't. So Cynthia is going to take you through the product advertising and how it can transform your business into a money-multiplying machine.

Dr Cynthia Porter

To explain the marketing formula, we're going use some of what we've already learned about the brain and how it works. You now know about brain wave frequencies and how they affect our decision-making. Now we're going to look at how brain waves affect the way people respond to marketing.

So let's start at the beginning, which means we look at what advertising is supposed to accomplish. Unfortunately, most business owners put together advertising without even stopping to think about what you're trying to achieve. We frequently see this in in the chiropractic field. Most doctors will copy what their competitors are doing, not realizing their competitors are copying from someone else. No one stops to think about what the prospective buyer wants.

So this will give you a foundation on how to put together your marketing and advertising, and give you a better understanding of why our advertising works. We're going to take a look first at what advertising is supposed to do.

First and foremost, advertising must grab the prospects attention. If it doesn't accomplish this, the rest of it doesn't matter.

And how do you grab their attention? You've got to give them hope you can solve a problem or fulfill a desire. If you can give someone hope that their problem can be resolved, they will have a driving force to use your product.

Once you have given them hope, you have to prove beyond a shadow of a doubt their hopes will be fulfilled.

In our own marketing we do what's called salesmanship in print. This concept is as old as advertising itself, but it has changed dramatically since the invention of television. Most people don't realize how much television changed the way marketing is done, and how it has hurt small businesses like the chiropractic clinic.

Finally, your marketing must make an offer of some kind. It should be low risk and an easy action to take. If you don't tell your prospects what to do, they will do what they've always done...think, ponder and procrastinate.

This is why I've often told rooms full of chiropractors that 95percent of their profession's ads suck. What I mean is they suck the profits out of the business. I'm not singling out chiropractic ads. Small business advertising in general is poorly conceived and improperly executed.

There are big, big mistakes being made in advertising merely because nobody is thinking in terms of what happens in the brain when you're looking at advertising.

Consequently, what we see is a world full of lousy advertising. Ads that fail to get anyone's attention soon become wallpaper, and if your ad is wallpaper, it sells nothing.

Marketing experts agree that you have about three seconds for any advertising to get and hold somebody's attention. You have to understand, people are bombarded with information today. In fact, they say we encounter more information in a single day than our great grandparents did in an entire lifetime. Through this dizzying array of information, we've got to find a way to stand out.

We need to prove to prospective patients why they should buy our product or service, and this is where most chiropractors fall short. Again, when we copy what other chiropractors are doing—images of the spine or a back in distress—prospects see the same thing over and over again. How can they distinguish what makes you better or worse, or any different from any other chiropractor?

Moreover, most chiropractic advertising fails to give anyone a reason to take action. Unfortunately this also means they fail at making money. Doctors will often say to me, "I've tried the newspaper, Cynthia, it didn't work, I've tried television it doesn't work, and I've tried radio it doesn't work."

Usually it boils down to the message being the problem, not necessarily the media. I can tell you, for our clinic, we use all of those methods and it works astonishingly well to the tune of about $150,000 a month. So as long as we have the right message, delivered in a way that awakens our potential prospect's brain, then the media is going to work for us.

Why are so many businesses doing it wrong?

There are two reasons businesses are doing it wrong. First, as mentioned earlier, a lot of business owners are emulating their competitors. Second, they are trying to do their advertising the way the national companies do. National companies make fortunes on TV advertising, but they create what is called image advertising. This came about out of necessity. At the dawn of television, broadcasters sold sponsorships, and they would usually have five minutes to educate the audience about their product, the way they used to do in print.

As TV became more prevalent, broadcasters kept narrowing down the amount of time advertisers had to tell their story, until the standard became 30 seconds, which is the length of most commercials today.

During the glory days of network advertising—before cable and pay channels came on the scene—they had such a large captive audience that big companies only had to put their brand name on the screen and their products sold. As time went on and the television market expanded, advertising agencies had to get creative. They learned to use cute and clever images, jingles and sounds to grab their prospects attention. Again, as long as the brand was built, people bought the products in droves.

So this image advertising, which was brought about through television, is now how everyone thinks it's done, but it will never work for you. Even if you were to hire one of the top New York ad agencies and they created a clever, award-winning advertising campaign, it would probably make you little or no money because you don't have a multi-billion dollar budget like McDonald's, Pepsi, and GM do.

You need to bring it back to salesmanship in a way that makes you stand out. You have something unique and different from any competitor out there—and that's what you need to focus on.

This is one of the opportunities Brain-Based Wellness affords you. For example, when it comes to weight loss, everyone is working on the body but nobody is working on the brain. People who are struggling to lose weight are desperate for something different and they inherently know they have eating problems that stem back to problems in their thinking, and that's where they get stuck. They have no idea how to change their thinking, so they bounce from one diet to the next. In marketing, we would call Brain-Based Wellness for weight-loss a unique selling proposition. It's what makes you stand out from all the rest.

Instead of image advertising, we use the formula devised by direct response marketers. This is going back to the same stuff direct mail giants have been doing for years, and believe it or not, 95 percent of the sales happen through direct response advertising; this is also the case on television.

What does direct response advertising do?

Direct response advertising produces a direct, immediate and measurable response; measurable is the key term here. You've got to have a way to be able to measure the response you're getting from the advertising you are conducting; otherwise you could end up throwing away a lot of money quickly. I'm sure if you're like us, and almost every small business out there, your budget for marketing is limited, you've got to make sure what you're doing is measurable or you could end up spending your entire marketing budget and getting little to no return. Direct response marketing also gives you an opportunity to tell a story or prove your case. Anytime something new comes onto the marketplace, there is a story to go with it. Dr Patrick Porter and I have been providing brain/mind-based wellness services since the 80s, so we have the opportunity to not only tell our story, but also prove to people this will give them a different result from anything else they tried in the past. Direct response advertising does this for us.

You want your prospects to take action now. Just getting somebody to remember your name isn't going to do it for a small business. Again, you've probably got a small budget so you have to have the ability to get people to say, "Yes, I want to find out more now!"

Separate yourself from the competition

You have probably found that most of the time chiropractors are setting themselves up where other chiropractors are already based and operating. So you have this geography issue where it's easy for people to find someone else right down the block. When people choose a chiropractor based on geography, it's only because in their minds you are doing the exact same thing as the chiropractor down the street or across town. You're not setting yourself apart from them. The best thing you have to promote yourself is with the word 'chiropractor' above the door. There's nothing there to separate you from the competition and there's no reason for anyone to choose you over someone else. The best you can hope for is getting people who walk by to notice you. This is no way to run a business. It's why we need to work on targeting your advertising so you can achieve the maximum results for every dollar spent.

The trust barrier

So since this book is all about discussing the human brain, we're going to talk a bit about the brain of the buyer. We need to ask ourselves, what state do people need to be in to make a decision? Then we need to ask, what state are they in when they encounter our advertising? In advertising we call this the trust barrier.

The trust barrier is a state of mind that's pervasive in our culture and has been created by brand advertising. It has to do with the person's inability to determine whether any business product or service is better or worse than any other. In this scenario, people feel like they don't have control, so they think, procrastinate, and comparison-shop. But what happens when somebody gets on the Internet and starts Googling? They could be there for ten days and still not begin to touch all the search results!

So you have to provide them enough information for them to feel they don't have to go out and comparison shop. Fortunately, with Brain Based Wellness, you have something no one else in your market is offering. In marketing, we call this a unique selling proposition and there's nothing more powerful for your business than to have something different from what all of your competitors are doing. Your goal is to get people to the point where they think, I'd have to be crazy to do business with anybody else.

Most businesses attempt to break through the trust barrier with creativity, humor and repetition. This chapter is about making sure that you know better. Unless you're promoting adult beverages, success in advertising is rarely about about being cute, clever and creative.

Take Super Bowl advertising as an example. During this four-hour span you see the best of what the advertising world has to offer, and they often do a great job of creating cute, clever and memorable spots. But here's the problem. Polls taken after the Super Bowl show that, while people often remember the ad, they don't remember the product the spot was promoting.

A few years ago, there was a Super Bowl commercial called "Herding cats." This was during the dot com era when dollars spent for Super Bowl advertising was at an all time high. The airtime for this one-minute commercial was about $4 million and certainly a few million more was spent on production. Yet only 5 percent of people polled the next day could remember the name of the company that spent those millions.

This is why chiropractors must get past this notion that our marketing and advertising has to be creative; it doesn't. What it has to be is successful in getting people to take action. What it has to do is get the message across that what you have to offer is a way to fix their problems.

The marketing equation

Fortunately, there is a marketing equation that accomplishes just this. It's a formula based on unchanging true principles, it works like arithmetic and as long as we know the principles we can always complete the equation; this means marketing doesn't have to be a guessing game.

One of the things I have given you is a way to test your advertising before you ever spend time and money on running ad. Instead of just throwing things against the wall, and seeing how cute and clever you can get, we're going to take you step-by-step through this unchanging principle. If all of those components are there, there's a good chance you're going to have a winner ad. You may have to test a few components to get maximum return, but for the most part, you're going to have a winner.

Success in advertising means activating the brains of individuals as they are thinking about their problems and searching for solutions. So let's delve into the brain of "Polly Prospect."

We're going to use three major concepts here and these go back to what Dr. Porter has already taught you about brain wave activity. This little marketing lesson is also going to help you understand a little bit more about how the brain operates in its different brainwave frequencies. So in relation to advertising, we're going to discuss alpha mode, beta mode and the reticular activating system.

Alpha mode

By now most of you understand what the alpha brain wave frequency is all about. You know the alpha frequency is important for creativity, for people to have focus, stay relaxed, calm, balanced and all the other benefits of alpha. However, in advertising we don't want our prospect to be in alpha mode because it primarily happens at the unconscious level. When people are in alpha mode, the brain is on autopilot. Routines and habits are formed or stem from alpha mode. When people are in alpha, and their beta brain wave activity is lower than their alpha, they are unaware of what they are doing or thinking. On average, people spend around 25percent of their waking hours in a dominant state of alpha. This is the brain's natural downtime. Today, one of the major problems we are seeing is people are having a harder time getting to alpha mode because they are over-stimulated. This means they aren't giving their brains the time needed to sort through the information with which it's constantly being bombarded. This is when chronic stress, fear, frustration, and all the negative habits start cropping up.

If you are not convinced that 25 percent of waking hours are spent in the virtually unconscious state of alpha, next time you are driving down the road and stop at a light, just look to your right and your left and look at people's faces. You'll soon see that at least 25 percent of the time people will have that glazed over look associated with alpha dominance. It's just like when you find yourself having driven to work and arriving without knowing how you got there.

If people are in alpha, how well are you going to get their attention? The answer is, probably not at all. So when it comes to advertising, you need your prospect's brain out of alpha mode. For example, when you see a billboard multiple times, it soon becomes like wallpaper to the brain. Even when the message changes, you will be oblivious to it—unless there is something there that triggers your reticular activating system, which we'll discuss in a moment.

This explains why consumers become oblivious to nearly all advertising messages and you have no chance to sell at that point. So you've got to devise something to grab people's attention.

Beta mode

We're now going to look at the beta mode. As you know beta is the wide-awake, alert state of consciousness. When somebody is in beta mode, they will consciously notice your advertising.

When your prospects are in this mode, they are also actively seeking out information on products and services. In other words, this is when somebody is paying attention. Maybe they are seeking ways to help them lose weight. If so, there will be a conscious awareness of anything relating to their problem. They are looking for a solution to help them in their goal, so when they see marketing that addresses this problem, it's going to register for them and they're going to pay attention.

Keep in mind that 95 percent of the brain is engaged in unconscious activity, while only 5 percent of the brain operates consciously. In a moment when we delve into the reticular activating system, you will start to understand how you can get people to snap into beta mode.

When prospects are in beta mode, they are in the right mode to allow them to absorb all the relevant information to make the best decision. One of the things I am known for is long copy advertising. I tend sell by telling stories. And I will use as many words as it takes to make sure I get the story across in the most compelling way.

This may go against everything you've previously thought about advertising, as many people think it needs to be quick, snappy and to the point. Over the years I've had many people say to me, No one is going to read all of that." My answer is this: If what the prospect is reading is helping them to better understand their problem and to get guidance toward a solution, then they will read every single word of it.

To prove my point, I used to have my evaluators (salespeople) ask prospects how much of the advertising they actually read. Invariably, if they got to the point of sitting in our clinic, they will say, "I read it all." Oftentimes they will pull a handful of my ads out of their purses and say, "Look, I've been carrying these around, I've read every single one over and over and I've finally made the decision to come in."

This proves people will read copy if they believe it's going to lead them to a solution. So if you were to look at the marketing we've developed for BBW, you would see a long introductory letter, because we have a story to tell and we need to prove that what we are saying happens actually happens. We most prove that Brain Based Wellness works.

Reticular Activating System

The reticular activating system is the subconscious ability your brain has to continually scan the environment around you without you being consciously awareness of it. In every moment, your brain is noticing dozens of things at once, even if you're actively engaged in something else. The reticular activating system is part of the internal system of the brain that keeps us safe, it's part of our survival mechanism. It's always going to be looking for are familiar or connected to you, and your brain is always comparing new information to what you already know.

For example, let's say you're a chiropractor, as most of you reading this book are, and you're sitting in a restaurant having lunch.

There's a group of people behind you are chatting away, and you're not paying attention the conversation at all...until you hear the word chiropractor. And all of a sudden, you're in their conversation. Consciously you weren't paying attention but your brain picked up familiar word and there you were, all of a sudden engaged in their conversation, "Oh," the brain says, "what do they have to say about chiropractors?"

Another good example of the reticular activating system is in the action of driving. When you're driving down the road in that 25 percent of your day where you're in alpha mode, daydreaming or thinking about what you're going to have for dinner, you're not consciously driving your car. But if you're not driving the car, who is? Well, there's another level of your mind driving your car, and it's called the reticular activating system. You've driven so many times and so well that you formed a habit. You are on autopilot.

But what happens when a car suddenly comes up alongside you and starts to pull into your lane? You've barely even seen the car, but in a split second, you're reticular activating system snapped you out of alpha mode and brought you into beta mode so you can handle the situation.

Next let's say that your car breaks down and you decide it's time to purchase a new one. You find a model that you love from the moment you set eyes on it. You think you'll be the only one on the road driving this beautiful car. You buy the car, and...

All of a sudden, you start seeing your car everywhere. Why? Because now it's familiar, so your reticular activating system will start spotting the car even when you're not consciously looking at other cars on the road.

The reticular activating system is a powerful part of the brain, and something we're going to use to help make our advertising do what it's supposed to do: grab people's attention!

The reticular activating system is always scanning your environment for that which is:

- Familiar
- Dangerous
- Incongruent

What's in it for me?

The next aspect of marketing we're going to cover is what we call WIIFM. You may have heard this before. It stands for, "What's in it for me?"

The truth is, people are inherently self-involved. They are always searching for whatever is going to help them to be happier, healthier, enjoy life more, or get free of pain. People make emotional decisions and then justify it with logic. People do not make rational decisions. It's just the way we are wired. Even some of the most rational people still fall into this emotional blind.

A good example is why do people by candy? We know candy is harmful to our bodies, we know it causes weight gain, blood sugar problems, and even diabetes, yet we still buy candy despite what we know logically about it. We buy it for the emotional benefit we get, the immediate gratification when we eat it, the taste, the sensation and all of the emotional links to past good times when we ate candy. Maybe the fun Halloween they had, the holiday treats or whatever it might be. All of these emotional triggers tell us to buy candy even when our logical mind knows it's not good for us and it's going to cause weight gain.

As marketers, we need to trigger the "What's in it for me?" response. So many businesses fall down on the job when it comes to advertising because they are so busy talking about themselves or their company that they fail to consider what the prospect wants. I'm going to show you what I mean in a minute.

When I do marketing training for chiropractors, I invite them to bring their advertising with them. Most of the time when we go through their brochures, all they talk about is how long they've been in this business, provide a list of the kinds of treatment they offer, and try to convince the people that they are great chiropractor. Again, when we do what our competitors are doing, we end up talking about ourselves rather than talking about the prospects and the benefits they will get by choosing you as a chiropractor.

The marketing equation

There are four elements to the Direct Response equation; this is what we're going to need to do to snap our prospects into beta.

The marketing equation

First of all we have to interrupt them from whatever they are thinking or doing. We must snap them out of alpha mode so we can then engage them. Once we have their attention, we must get them to remain interested. We then use our salesmanship to prove that we can follow through with the claims we're making. We must show them that our services have already worked for others in the same position as they are in. We might show them research; maybe use testimonials, facts, figures, and hard data. Then we're going to make an offer. We're going to ask the prospect to take the next step. Most chiropractors completely miss getting people to take action right now.

Interrupt

So step one is to interrupt with ad style, headlines and photos. These are the three components of advertising. I don't care if you are doing a radio spot, TV website, landing page, or a newspaper ad. Whatever it is, the three components you need to have are style, headlines and photos to interrupt the prospect.

With the headline, you need it to be bold and attention grabbing. If you use the name of your practice as a headline, when you're testing your ad you're already going to find out you haven't done too well. The name of your business is not a headline. Slogans are not headlines. A headline is information you tell the prospect. Headlines say, "This is how I'm going to help you fix the problem in your life. I'm going to give you a way out of your pain."

Another way to do headlines is to use editorial style, which means that you emulate news stories. You can do this in newsprint, in your promotional materials or online. There's no better way to get people to take what you're saying at face value than to emulate news stories to make an advertisement look like an editorial; this is what we mean by editorial styles.

With photos, there's a reason why the weight loss industry still uses BEFORE and AFTER photos. People are fascinated to see the transformation in others. It also helps them to visualize themselves, and their own BEFORE and AFTER photos.

Remember, we have three seconds to get a person's attention, and the way to do it is either with a big bold headline or with photos. This immediately tells the person what your business is about. BEFORE and AFTER photos work so well with weight loss because people instantly know it works, it snaps them out of alpha and into beta mode.

The headline itself is an advertisement for the advertisement, which is why it's the key component to your ad. I will typically write between 25 and 100 different headlines before I settle on the right one. I do this is for any advertisement I am writing or anytime I'm doing a long copy sales letter online. I can spend a whole day just on the headlines because it has to appeal to the reader's self-interest.

Create a sense of urgency. We need to make the prospect want more. We also need to be unique and extremely specific. This is where I see a lot of people falling down on the job. I call these lazy headlines. If there is no specificity, if it's vague, boring, or full of platitudes, it will not to snap anybody out of anything. It just becomes wallpaper and no one even sees it. In that case, you may as well keep your dollars in your bank account.

As I mentioned earlier, slogans are not headlines, but this is what I often see chiropractors do, primarily because they are trying to be clever. Here are some examples I pulled right out of a local magazine for the Bay area: "Affordability now comes with a view." This ad could be for just about anything. It could be someone selling a home, a vacation or even a timeshare. There's nothing there to snap somebody into beta mode.

Here is another one I see all the time: "Serving the Bay area since 1957." If you write something to put into an ad, the first thing you need to do is ask yourself, Who cares?

Chances are, no one is going to care about when a business was founded. You might want to say this later on in your copy when you're proving that you can deliver the goods, but it's certainly not a headline, nor does it belong in the interrupt section.

Here's another one, again pulled right out of a magazine. This was also on the ad as though it were the headline: "Home of fast, friendly courteous service." This is another test you're going to do. I call this the replacement test. If you can take your slogan, or what you call your headline, and replace it with any other business or any of your competitors, and it would say the same thing, then you've got to change it because it's not going to speak to your business specifically. So hopefully you're seeing now not only do these slogans not serve as headlines, but they aren't even slogans in my opinion.

This is what we see in advertising all the time, and it's why I said earlier 95 percent of all ads suck the profits right out of your business.

Think in terms of hot buttons. We all know the expression to, "Push somebody's buttons." Well, that's just what you want to do here. If someone is smoker, he or she has likely tried to quit many times before. You've got to let them know you can deliver a viable solution they haven't tried before. This is not the patch. This is not nicotine chewing gum. This is a new, big idea for how we're going to help somebody to stop smoking. In a moment, I'm going to share with you some 'stop smoking' headlines.

David Ogilvy, one of the greatest copywriters of all time, said headlines are read five times more than the copy below them. This tells you at least four out of five headlines fail because they don't pull people into the copy. Your headline has got to grab your prospect by the lapels, push those emotional hot buttons, and be unique and ultra-specific.

This is a great headline I found in a magazine, and you'll notice it's long. It's okay to have a long headline if you have some photos and make it clear what we are talking about here:

Finally a way to make serious money in real estate without ever buying or selling property, and without risking 1 thin dime of your own money.

This tells people exactly what the ad is going to be about, and anybody who's been thinking about getting into real estate, is going to be drawn in by two specific things. First, they don't have to buy or sell any property so there's no risk; they don't have to risk a dime of their own money. Second, it's different from what everybody else out there is talking about in relation to buying, selling or flipping real estate.

This is a strong headline. One of the ways I know its strong is because I've seen this ad repeatedly within same publication, which tells you it's working, or at least most of the time if they're tracking.

Now we also use photos to interrupt. A picture tells a thousand words. Your photo has to show your prospect what your ad is about, which BEFORE and AFTER photos do perfectly. It needs to push emotional hot buttons, it must be unique, and of course demonstrate the self-interest appeal; people have a natural interest in other people.

I recommend using people in your photos whenever you possibly can. People love to look at other people. It's why you see magazines full of beautiful men and women.

Engage

Once we have their attention, we have to keep them engaged. We do this using a lead, photo captions, and sub-headings. So if we've got an attention grabbing headline, the next thing we have to do is get them to keep reading. We keep people engaged when we give them hope, make a promise, and paint mental pictures. This is where we expound upon the big idea we have initially set forth in our headline.

Subheadings and photo captions do this well. Keep the reader moving through the copy; people will read long copy if they believe it's going to get them to an end-result they are looking for. You've got to keep the promise alive. These are all pieces of the puzzle that make advertising extraordinarily effective.

Prove

The next thing you're going to do is prove what you're telling them is true. This is where you get into the juicy details, and this is where you have to be ultra-specific. Again, just saying, "Research shows this happens," doesn't work. You need to say, "This specific research shows this specifically happened."

In the following example, I'm going to show you the difference specificity can make. Even if you are not a smoker, you will feel the difference in how you respond to those particular headlines. So here we go, which one rings more true?

We've helped thousands of people stop smoking

This headline sounds pretty good and it certainly tells people what you're doing is helping people stop smoking, so it does a pretty good job of at least letting them know what the ad is about.

But how is this for a better headline:

2,758 people can't be wrong.
They've stopped smoking with hypnosis and you can, too!

This is just to give you an idea of how when you're ultra-specific it becomes much more believable. Lazy headlines don't capture anyone's attention. Now if I were to read this headline, I would think, 2,758 is a lot of people, maybe there is something to this. Now, when I get into reading further, you'd better prove to me you're telling the truth, otherwise I'm gone. So when you're ultra-specific in your headline, you also have to be ultra-specific in your copy.

When we are talking about getting into people's reticular activating systems, it boils down to snapping them into beta mode, getting them to pay attention and keeping their attention.

For clarification, we are going to use an example of a protein bar, which is a product you want to sell. We start by remembering that people always have at the back of their mind, "What's in it for me?" For this reason, we are going to sell benefits, not features.

Let's say a feature of your protein bars is it has metabolic enhancers. First of all, does anybody know what a metabolic enhancer is? Probably not, unless you're in the protein bar industry, but a metabolic enhancer helps to burn fat while you are asleep; so now you've got an exciting benefit. Of course later on, you're going to want to explain how you know and how you can prove these metabolic enhancers burn fat while you're asleep.

Another feature is added fiber. We all know fiber is good for us and we need it, but it doesn't mean much to me. However, if you tell me I can eat this protein bar and stay full for four hours, now we've got a benefit statement, because one of the things I suffer with is constant cravings and being hungry between meals. This is going to keep me full for four hours, now we've got a benefit I can get on board with.

"Rated number 1 in taste" sounds like a great feature, but, again, rated number 1 by whom? Ask yourself these specific questions as you're writing your copy, rated number 1 in taste means nothing to me. I don't know who did the rating; I don't know what I was compared to, so it's just wallpaper as I said earlier.

But if we say 9 out of 10 surveyed said, "Better tasting than a Snickers bar," now we've painted a mental picture for somebody and you've got their taste buds going. They're going to be tempted to at least try this bar, which they know can burn fat while they sleep, keep them full for 4 hours, and tastes better than a Snickers. We're going to get people to want to try this product by turning features into benefits. Hopefully, this is starting to all come together and is helping you understand how to influence the brain in order to get people motivated to try your product or service.

Offer

I mentioned earlier the unique selling proposition; the question you want to ask yourself is 'is it irresistible?' Put yourself in your prospect's shoes. If you are talking about weight loss, think in terms of how you'll probably all encounter patients who are overweight and who have struggled with their weight for years, with on again-off again dieting. Know the pain they are in, step into their shoes, and think about what they might need or want, then ask yourself, "Is my offer irresistible?"

When it comes to weight loss services, one of the things Brain Based Wellness offers you as a unique selling proposition. You can offer something completely different from what other people are doing for weight loss.

There's nobody else addressing the mental side of the weight loss problem. Everybody is doing the same thing, calories in - calories out, another way of dieting. There's a million ways of dieting, but if you don't change your thinking, how likely is it you're going to keep the weight off? The same is true with stress, chronic pain, stopping smoking, and addiction. Whatever it might be, we have this unique selling proposition: We're treating these issues where they started in the first place. It's in the brain, not the body.

There is one offer that is the most irresistible out there, and some of you may already have it in your mind, but this irresistible offer is what's called free. Anytime you can give someone an opportunity to try it for free, typically it's the most irresistible offer. One of my favorite ways I have of inviting people to try something for free is I will say, "We are so confident in our results we're willing to let you come in and find out for yourself absolutely free." That's a powerful statement right there.

The thin line

In marketing our goal is always to reach as many people as possible, but we need to be aware of what is called the thin line. This is something I do a whole day's training on, but I want to give you the general idea of the thin line here to help you understand how direct response marketing works for both immediate response and long-term practice building.

The thin line refers to a thin area in time when people are ready to do something about their problem right now. Using weight loss for an easy example, we know that 65 percent of the American population is overweight right now, but at this particular moment in time, maybe only 5 percent of that 65 percent is truly ready to do something about their weight problem. So the thin line is when somebody is ready to make a decision now.

When it comes to overweight people, there are more people in the thin line on Monday than any other day of the week. This is likely because the average diet lasts 72 hours. It starts on Monday and ends on Wednesday. During this window, the reticular activating system of overweight people will be more likely to notice a weight loss message. Therefore, our goal is to get people's attention when their reticular activating system is at its most powerful, which in this case is Monday. This is just one example of how we can work our advertising so we can capture the attention of as many people in the thin line as possible.

The Hopper System

Because of the thin line, direct response marketing will often use a two-step approach. Online marketers use this technique all the time.

Step one involves getting the prospect to acquire some bit of information from us for free. We now have their mailing or email address and we can continue to drip-market to them.

We call this our hopper system. The people in the hopper have expressed interest in the products but they weren't in the thin line—the right mindset—just yet. Now we continue to inform and educate the prospect about how we can fix their problem.

In this way, we can maximize the thin line people—our hot leads—while also maximizing those who were not in the thin line—our warm leads—when they see our advertising. By continually educating and marketing to these warm leads, you will be in the best position to get their business when they cross over into the thin line.

A lot of the marketing we provide to those who choose to engage in our Brain Based Wellness system follows this exact formula. We strive to appeal to "who's ready to buy now," and "who will buy in the future." Effective marketing will reach both.

Direct response marketers call this 2-step marketing, or sometimes they refer to it as giving prospects a baby-step, a simple little action they can take now, before they are ready to take the big action.

The guarantee

One of the other things we also recommend is a guarantee, but only you can legally do so in your state.

We recommend using a guarantee whenever possible because today's consumer is smart and savvy, but also skeptical. They've seen a lot of advertising that didn't live up to its promises. So one of the best things we can do is remove the risk. Of course, one of the best ways to do this is with a free offer. We're so confident in it, come in and find out for yourself—FREE!

In this situation, they have nothing to lose and everything to gain. But you can also offer a guarantee where they can try the program for one day or week—whatever makes sense to you—and if it doesn't help them with their problems, then you'll give them their money back. If they have nothing to lose and everything to gain, they will buy from you.

People often ask me, "Cynthia, where do I start?" I always recommend that you start where you are. You already have patients who know you, who trust you, who came to see you before for a reason. Now you go back to those same patients and let them know you something new to offer, something different than anything else out there, and by the way, I'm so confident in what I have to offer you, you can come in and try it for free

No matter how we are promoting Brain Based Wellness, we always use this formula.

I've visited dozens of chiropractic offices, and on thing I notice is that few take advantage of internal marketing strategies. In our clinic, you'll only find our walls lined with before/after photos, testimonials and posters with strategic headlines announcing the services we offer.

"Vanquish stress from your life!"

"Activate your fat-burning hormones!"

"End emotional eating!"

Even in the office, we are trying to push those emotional hot buttons to inspire patients to take action. For a lot of people, emotional eating is a big hot button. No matter how hard they try to diet, emotional eating trips them up.

You can start changing your marketing strategy today, and the best first step is to throw out all of the magazines and newspapers and get rid of everything in your office that might be a distraction. Then start slowly and systematically replacing until you have created what we call a results environment. Everywhere your patients look, they should see success. Start putting up posters, before/after photos, and testimonials. Put out brochures and flyers designed to trigger your patients' reticular activating system, inspiring them to take action now.

Summary

Too often advertising fails when small businesses try to brand like the big corporations with cute and clever slogans. Don't try to be a Super Bowl advertiser. Rather, educate your consumers. Teach them about why they've failed in the past and what it takes to succeed. Tell them the truth. When they are ready, they'll come and see you.

Focus all of your marketing on the customer and not the company. If a sentence starts with "I" or "We," figure out how to change it to "You." Tell you prospect, "This is how you are going to benefit," and, "This is how your life is going to improve." Talk about how you can improve your prospective patient's life and you'll be light years ahead of your competitors.

Later, when you're proving you can deliver on your promise, it is appropriate to list your credentials and accomplishments. But it's in your prove section, it's not your headline, it's not your lead, and it's not your primary copy. This is one of the most important changes you can make immediately with your practice style.

Assignment

Prepare your direct marketing list. Start by asking key questions.

What are your goals?

Who are you trying to reach?

What is that person's biggest problem?

What are his or her hot buttons?

Begin with your end in mind so you can be as specific as possible. You will need to go through this process for every type of problem area you are targeting. People for weight loss have different emotional hot buttons that people who need stress management or have sleeping problems.

When integrating a Brain Based Wellness system in your clinic, you will start repeating the process multiple times, your clinical results will get better, your marketing efforts will be better, you will attract lots more patients into your office, your retention will be better, your reputation will expand and grow and your profitability will go through the roof.

As we've said many times throughout this book, Bran Based Wellness is the ultimate back end in a chiropractic practice; it can be like a license to print money.

If you already have our Brain Based Wellness system in your office, or if you choose to become a BBW provider, start by offering free demos to the people on your list, but be sure to pre-frame them for the demo.

You know Mrs. Jones, you're an ideal candidate who will thrive from this Brain Based Wellness process to help you relieve and neutralize your stress. If you feel relaxed, centered, calm, peaceful, any of those types of responses, this will be a positive test showing that you will benefit greatly from the 12-week program that I will recommend. Continue your action plan for your personal brain health. What are the steps you're taking to put yourself back into balance, back into harmony, back into homeostasis so you can consistently and continuously show the best version of yourself each and every day? If you truly want to help your patients, this is an absolutely essential starting point for each and every one of us.

Take time each day to use the technology yourself, and expect miracles. Get a sense of how amazing this BBW is. It takes a little time, but as neurons fire together, they will wire together, and you will find yourself so much more centered and focused with better concentration. You'll no longer be a victim of the shiny objects in the room that distract you.

Hopefully by now we have brought to your attention how simple, obvious and how easy BBW is to implement in your practice. Start coupling BBW with chiropractic care and you'll be producing the most amazing clinical results ever.

Where the rubber hits the road is putting BBW into action, and that includes implementing a well thought out direct response marketing strategy. When you do, you're going to see some great results and that's what matters most.

CHAPTER

EIGHT

**Office systems and flow –
Your key to Maximum Profit**

Office systems and flow – Your key to maximum profit

In this chapter we are going to learn how to go deeper into implementing the system and how to work with the external marketing to assist you in your sales efforts. We're going to instruct you in detail on how to market and promote your Brain Based Wellness programs. We believe through these methods you can attract an unlimited number of new patients because you will begin to realize potential patients are everywhere.

You will learn how to use electronic media, newspapers and flyers; including flyers that we have already produced. You will learn more about in-house events and what we do, because this is a great way to attract new clientele or new patients into your practice. You will also learn to identify who in your office should be doing public speaking engagements if that is not something you are comfortable doing yourself. Finally, we will cover referral programs and what we have found works over the years to help build your practice.

We have a solid history of having forty percent of our clientele being referral based and we had between 160 and 170 people a day coming through our offices so we are fully equipped with the knowledge of how to help your office reach its fullest potential.

Converting your patient from chiropractic care to the Brain Based Wellness program

It's important to remember there is an endless well of clientele just waiting to take advantage of your services. Thinking for a moment about the community around you, remember: sixty five percent of the people out there in the community probably want to lose weight; between eighty five to a hundred percent of the people out there are stressed, literally, out of their mind. A healthy percentage of the population around you have difficulty falling asleep, staying asleep, or waking up refreshed. People are suffering from chronic pain conditions. There is no limit to the number of new patients you can draw into your business.

There are two categories of people. You have patients that are currently part of your practice but that you want to convert to your MindFit system in addition to their chiropractic care. And there are new patients that will come in for the MindFit program as a result of your advertising that you will want to convince to add chiropractic care. Keep in mind you will not convert a hundred percent of your patients either way, but if handled correctly, a large percentage can be convinced.

The key to doing this is to continually teach that all stress is ultimately brain stress, regardless of its physical, chemical or emotional nature, and that stress causes the brain to become imbalanced. The foundation to this is that regular chiropractic care will maximize the clinical outcome, the results, and how your patients will feel and function in the end. Every adjustment they receive reboots and rebalances the brain and normalizes and maximizes brain function. People who are already chiropractic patients will recognize this. Your job is to teach them how the MindFit program will benefit them by helping to negate their stress, reprogram their brain and allow their adjustments to retain longer.

We suggest you offer a complimentary consultation to current chiropractic patients to show them the MindFit and how it works. Demonstrate how stress has affected their health, and their ability to respond and heal. This is one of the most effective methods of advertising--letting people get a taste of what your product can do. Conversely, you can offer free chiropractic adjustments to MindFit patients as a convincer that the two programs work best together. We believe the two programs working in conjunction will give great clinical results, generate endless new patients, increase PVA and compliance, and dramatically improve your profitability and your reputation within your community.

Targeting new patients

With the Brain Based Wellness solution, you have over thirty different avenues you utilize to target your patients. Each week you can focus on one of the different target areas and talk about how your Brain

Based Wellness solution will help that particular area. We recommend using social media such as Facebook, YouTube and personal websites. You could also utilize a blog to help get your message out. Getting people to follow you on social media is basically free advertising and nothing is more powerful than word of mouth. Make sure when you have speaking engagements you mention any websites, blogs or Facebook pages to the people listening to you. You can be sure they will check you out and their friends will check you out as well.

We have also found that certain advertising mediums work well for certain programs. For example, advertising for stress reduction works better when presented in a seminar format than if you advertise in the newspaper. On the other hand, if you're advertising for weight loss, that works best when advertised in the newspaper.

When we're asked to give a local lecture or talk on a subject, we have found it's best to focus it on one specific area, whether it is a solution for insomnia, a pain-free solution, or just a general health solution. The talk should always be focused around those listeners and how you can help them. We always try to give them something they can do in the seminar so they take something away from it without having to come into the clinic but you also want to stress to them that the clinic offers much, much more that they are looking for.

We give away what we call "free tickets to ride" which we're going to talk about a little bit here. We give them out to every participant in the speaking engagement so when they come into the office, they're treated as they should be--as a VIP. We take them through the clinic, show them what we have to offer and give them a ride (demonstration) on the equipment. Or we give them a report of findings to establish where they are and what we might be able to do to help them the most. These speaking topics, even though you're going to give high value will also be used to bring new clientele into your clinic so you can support them with a real program.

Let me give you an example. We have a terrific doctor in The Master's Circle who started marketing inside his own practice. He put together an all-natural, doctor supervised 12-week weight loss program, and invited those patients who he thought would benefit from it and their guests to come to a presentation. This doctor had fifty people come in on a Monday night. He spoke for about thirty or forty minutes speaking about the reality of being overweight, about how obesity is creating major problems in our country and leading to comorbid conditions such as cancer, diabetes, and high blood pressure.

He told them he recognized there are many options out there for losing weight and about how most of those options don't work because they don't address the fundamental problem of how their brain functions and the emotional connection to food. He explained to the group how he had put together this twelve week program. Every week for twelve weeks he taught a thirty minute class on a different topic. He taught about things like portion control, foods to avoid, super foods to eat as much of as you like, why taking a thirty minute walk every night after dinner is one of the smartest activities you could do; simple, basic, fundamental things. He taught them how to replace one meal a day with an all-natural smoothie.

He told them in advance they should expect to lose one to three pounds a week and that they would use the MindFit system two times a week. He gave them an introductory price, prepaid for the twelve weeks for $1500. Thirty eight of the fifty people signed up on the spot. He collected over $50,000 that night. Twelve of those people were not current chiropractic patients, so he included in that price for them a chiropractic history and exam and most likely will convert nine or ten of those people to chiropractic care.

That's one simple example of how powerful and easy this is. You find the niche in the marketplace, set up a simple doctor-supervised, safe procedure. You set them up in a program, decide on a fair and reasonable fee using the guidelines and boundaries we have given you and get to work. The doctor from the example believes he can generate anywhere from $100,000-$150,000 per month in cash just using this system for these programs. This is in addition to his chiropractic income. He now is getting ready to launch a twelve week stress-reduction program and an insomnia program.

This is all basically common sense. Use the things you already know. Speak your patients' language. Use social media. Again, going back to our example doctor, he also recorded a simple two-minute video explaining his revolutionary twelve week, all natural, doctor-supervised weight loss program. He put it on YouTube and sent it out to his patients through Facebook and Twitter, and other similar online accounts. It is that simple. Remember, this is helping to solve a huge problem in your community. People are willing to pay for this solution. It is remarkable how profitable it can be and how large your practice can grow if you simply utilize the tools you already have.

Do we offer our patients a guarantee?

We have been asked by several of the doctors already using the program whether we offer our patients any kind of guarantee on the program. The answer is we can't ethically and morally guarantee results. What we can do is guarantee our services. One of the things offering a guarantee does is to take the risk off the table for the patient. It makes them more inclined to buy.

A guarantee works well, particularly with the stop smoking programs. We get tremendous results with this program, but there are going to be people who won't completely stop smoking in the time period we prescribe. Our guarantee is we will continue working with them until they do stop. Eventually they will stop. They just need a little more time and effort than other people. Those types of guarantees you can ethically make.

Here we're going to explain some of the options we have used. You don't have to use any of these, but we have found over the years they do work well. We have our patients sign the guarantees when they are completing the paperwork for the program.

For the Brain Based Wellness program we typically recommend a stick with it guarantee. What this guarantee provides is that when someone joins our program we are going to continue to work with them until they're happy with their results.

Now we're not going to give them one-on-one sessions and we are not going to personally record anything for them. They're going to come in and use the Brain Based Wellness system. They're going to come in and use the MindFit machine and listen to the audio-sessions you recommend. What we find is when they come in for these sessions, most people are happy anyway. The real issue is they want to know what happens in twelve weeks if they didn't get the results they were looking for.

Remember, you are not guaranteeing results. We can't guarantee their behavior or life choices. We can guarantee them they're going to get the education. What that does is gives them the ability—if they're not happy with their results—to retake the information. You don't have to pay for it again, but you can go through and re-experience it. We let people do that until they're happy. We find this part of the guarantee works well because a lot of people don't know about this kind of technology yet, so it gives them the chance to experience it and get the results they want. We also find that only about ten percent of the enrolled clients actually ever need to utilize this portion of our guarantee.

We actually prefer to sell them the optional program at the end, which we mentioned before in one of the earlier chapters. We sell them an add-on where they pay $85 to $100 per month for additional services in our clinic; but we leave it up to each clinic if they want to offer that option.

Offering any kind of ethical guarantee like the "we stick with it guarantee" is a phenomenal thing because it takes the indecision, stress, and the uncertainty out of the mind of the patient and that itself starts to contribute to their results. When people are experiencing stress and uncertainty they can't do their best work. They can't think clearly enough to make the right decisions. When you are in constant stress, you are in survival mode. It is impossible to learn or grow and it's impossible for them to make an informed decision. Offering this guarantee alleviates that stress for them, clearing the way for a good decision.

No doubt for some of you reading this your left brain is activating here and you're hearing the mantra of "what if, what if, and what if?"

Yes, a small percentage of your clientele who will invoke the guarantee. So what if they do? It's not a big deal. The important factor is having a happy client who follows through with their program. Those are the clients that get results, and refer friends and family to your clinic.

Expanding your market reach

Now, you've done your seminar. You've had clients come in and sign up. What do you do then to expand your marketing potential? One of the most effective things we did in our centers was what we called patient events. Normally we offer four patient events in a year—starting at the beginning of the year in January. The theme of this particular event usually has something to do with re-engaging in your life, rejuvenating your life and getting ready for the New Year. Almost everyone sets goals on January 1st for the New Year. We do an event to help them to activate those goals. The point here is we give them a chance to bring family and friends with them to the event—possible future patients.

We also hold events in the spring and summer. Those events are geared toward helping them to learn more about their brain and how it works and functions. This is usually a two or three hour event and again they can bring family and friends with them.

In addition to patient events, we also offer family and friends events in the form of discounts available for the family and friends of patients already enrolled in our programs. Most of our patients have a family member or a friend who could benefit from your services. Why not make it easier to get them in the door? We will typically give them between twenty five to fifty percent off a program for introducing an additional family member and a twenty five percent discount for friends that come in. For example, if you have a husband and wife sign up together for a program, we might have the husband pay full price for his program but give the wife fifty percent off of hers. They are going to get much better results working together.

If you only have one source of revenue, one way people can come in, or you're mining all of your prospects from your existing chiropractic patients, you're going to eventually run out of new people. Bringing Brain Based Wellness into your clinic is going to open up a pool of new resources to bring into your clinic giving you a wider net you can spread out in your community to bring people in and those people will benefit from not only Brain Based Wellness but from your chiropractic care as well.

Best Times to Advertise--the Marketing Calendar

During our many years operating centers in different parts of the country, we have found we would make two thirds of our money for the year between January and June. This is the time of year you're going to get the biggest push of people between New Years' resolutions and getting ready for bikini season. If you're going to experiment with new advertising you've never tried before, usually January, February, and March is a good time to do this because you'll have the maximum number of people in the thin line.

This is where your hopper system becomes important. Remember, just because the person didn't buy today doesn't mean they won't buy in the future. Only about five to ten percent of the people who hear your message will pick up the phone and call you today. That's why companies like McDonalds and other major brands advertise constantly. They want to stay in the forefront of consumer's minds. We call this "top of mind awareness." It's not always about who shows up today, so you want to have a system in place.

July and August are sometimes not good advertising times for lifestyle programs such as those in the Brain Based Wellness system. We advertise through the whole summer as long as the advertising continues to work. Don't be afraid to pull something that's not working. If we have some type of advertising we're doing and traffic slows down or even stops, we pull it because we know that direct response advertising should draw them in the same week. If it's going to work, it's going to work this week. You're going to get the calls. You're going to get people coming in to your seminars. When it doesn't work, it means you need to take some time off from that advertising.

This is when we recommend you market your hopper system. This is when we do postcard mailings, and direct mail. We also do email almost every week. We normally do not offer general discounts on our programs unless it's July through August or December. Those are the only three months we would ever offer a discount to new patients (not including friend and family discounts) because normally there is no reason to do so. There are plenty of people out there willing to pay the full amount, and you never want to end up competing on price.

You will want to give a discount to family and friends as stated above, and possibly during live events, but for your regular newspaper, radio or TV advertising, you would not offer such a discount. We only recommend discounts through a mailer or through somebody who's already contacted us. These are people who have already acknowledged the problem, but may need a nudge in the right direction to get them to take action. This gives you a way to follow up with those people.

September to Thanksgiving is another time period where there is a big boom in the self-help industry. This will be the time period to beef up your advertising again. Kids are going back to school. Moms have time on their hands. People want to get in shape or get their lives together before the holidays or reduce their stress before big family gatherings. This is the time to get the word out about your programs. However, we make sure to stop advertising the week before Thanksgiving. It's our last big hurrah. We typically don't advertise Thanksgiving week, taking a break until December. Then, during December you will want to reactivate your hopper system. You will find oftentimes that during those first two weeks of December you can get a good return on the hopper system offers that you invest in.

When we were running our franchise system; we used to purchase and have all of our marketing set in place for one year in advance. Things would run like a machine allowing us to take time off and know that the marketing portion of our business was being taken care of all year long. This is something we advocate to the doctors in our system now. Set up a yearly calendar, a marketing calendar for an entire year at a time. Know what the busy times of year for your clinic will be. Hit the advertising heavier in the early months, lighten up during the summertime because that's when people are on vacation and are less apt to come in or even see your advertising.

Some clinics may find that they never experience a slow down period. Because you also have chiropractic in your office, you have people coming in all year round. They will see other patients benefiting from the Brain Based Wellness programs and want to experience that for themselves. As long as you are seeing a return on your investment, keep the advertising going. Don't just advertise for the sake of advertising. Devise a way to monitor how effective your advertising is and adjust accordingly. We recommend seeing a minimum of a three to one return. If you are spending $1000 on an ad you should see at the bare minimum a $3000 return on that investment or it's not worth running. The good thing about advertising is you are able to look at trends. Media avenues experience slow periods as well. When this happens you can advertise for less. So pay attention to this when you speak to your advertising representatives in the different mediums.

We believe the biggest market out there is the weight loss market. For this market the best days to advertise are Sunday, Monday and Tuesday. People tend to start diets early in the week and lose resolve later in the week. Your prospects will be aware they ate too much over the weekend. Their pain is intensified, and where there's pain, there is profit.

If the average diet lasts around 72 hours you have Monday, Tuesday and maybe Wednesday. The remaining four days they are not focusing on diet. They are not even going to see, hear or engage in your advertising. It could be right there in front of them but they're not going to see it because their mindset is not in a place to make a decision. So don't waste money on an audience that is not paying attention.

Landmines in advertising

We're now going to go into what we call the "landmines in advertising." This was covered some in the previous chapter, but we will go a little more in depth now. Advertising for Brain Based Wellness is different than advertising for chiropractic. You want to move away from how great you are as an individual and focus more on how great the program is. You want this program to run without you, so whether you are there or not your clinic can make money. The appeal has to be about the end-result. When you read our example advertising you will notice that it is results based, not doctor based.

We don't talk about how great doctor so and so is, because it doesn't matter. What matters is how great these results are for the people using the system. That's what makes the system work. You want the system to work with you and work when you're not there.

We also want to avoid technical terms. When you introduce this program, of course you can use words like Brain Based Wellness. It's a little less of a mouthful than saying "we use frequency following response and we train the brain to go through different brain wave states." That can become too convoluted and the message gets confusing. The key is to keep it simple.

There's an old saying in advertising and marketing which says, "Speak to Ms. O'Grady because the Colonel's lady won't mind." What that means is speak to the common man because the more educated will understand anyway. If you try to get too complicated, some people who want to use your services will feel offended because they won't understand the nomenclature being used by you as a doctor. If you want to achieve great results, keep it simple.

We also do not recommend you change the copy in any of our provided advertising. A lot of research went in to the way the copy reads. It works. There is so much boring copy out there and quite honestly, people won't read it. To hook your audience your advertising must be specific. That's why we provide you with a lot of the marketing material. It's bulleted. It has a point. At the end of it, it's going to say, "take action." Unless you have a lot of marketing experience, we simply don't recommend you try to write your own ads. Let the experts who have a proven track record do that for you. We know how to get results.

We have also learned that we don't talk about our own credentials in the advertising. It's just the wrong thing to do. Our advertising focuses on the client and what we can do to help them get the results they are looking for. Remember, we're trying to get that prospective patient in the door. We don't use kitsch or humor. Leave that for the giant companies like Coca-Cola. They can get away with it. You can't.

It's important when you're doing your advertising you're focusing on one corner of the market at a time. When you're marketing for a weight loss client, you want to focus on the results you're going to get with weight loss. When you're advertising for the Insomnia Program, you want to focus on insomnia only. People are looking for reasons to take action, and the more things you start listing, the more people are going to be convinced that, "Nobody can do all of these things." They will, however, believe you can do the one thing they need, and when it's their time, they're going to come to you. Remember the 1+1=0 rule. That means if you're trying to advertise two things at the same time, you're going to get zero response. You want to be laser-specific and you don't want to be linking all of these things together. It's confusing and once you confuse your potential patient, they will generally take no action.

Taking out a newspaper ad

If you haven't purchased a newspaper ad before, there are some tips we feel are important to share with you. We've purchased between $30-40 million worth of newspaper ads over the years for our different businesses and franchises so we have learned a few things about what works and what doesn't work.

We have also found that over the years newspaper ads are getting less and less expensive. Just to give you an idea, in 2005 in the

Bay Area it cost us almost $8000 for a full page ad. Today we've been able to negotiate the same ad for a third of that. Newspapers are willing to negotiate on the price—and there should always be a negotiation. You should never take the first price you're given. Work with your media reps to get the absolute best price.

When the media rep comes in, understand that they work for you, not the other way around. In most newspapers the rep doesn't get paid unless you buy something from them. So you have some leverage. Use them to get the best deal you can from that newspaper. Take the time to get to know your rep, set up some one-on-one time with them. Make sure you're setting up an account that is going to work for them and for you.

The best way to negotiate discounts on advertising is through that rep. Sometimes the newspapers will give you a discount on one run but they also do what they call "repeat runs," which means you're going to run one ad one week and then the same ad the next week. Typically you'll get those two ads for about forty five percent of the price it would cost to run just the one ad on its own. There are different discounts that are available and it's worth it to ask about them.

We never recommend you sign up for any kind of long term deal with a newspaper. If you do, it's important to understand all advertising should have a two-week cancellation clause. Make sure you ask for it and that it's put into any contract. If the advertising isn't working you need to have a way of getting out of the contract. Otherwise you're wasting money. Occasionally we have found that once we're in a market for a period of time and we know what is working correctly we are comfortable signing up for a full one-year deal to get greater discounts on the volume of ads we normally run. Just tread on this type of path carefully.

Another way to find out about discounts a newspaper may offer is watching other business's advertisements. If you begin to see certain ads in the paper over and over again, sometimes it's worth calling them up and asking them about it. First of all, it's a good idea to complement them on their ad, "'Wow, I like your ad in the Journal.

I think it's wonderful. Could you tell me a little bit about what you pay for it?" You'd be surprised how many people will tell you what they're paying for the ad. Sometimes you can use this information to leverage a better price for yourself.

You need to do your research so you can ask for and get the newspaper to give you the greatest discount they can. They can't discount you any greater than anyone else but you should work to get the best deal the newspaper has available. Any money you can save in advertising will directly contribute to your profit at the end of the month.

Most newspapers will do your ad layout for you. If they do the layout it's important to refer to the checklist we have given you so you can rate your ad before it gets printed. I have lost count of the number of times we've had our franchisees run ads in the newspaper with our center's phone number in it. Obviously they didn't review the checklist and as a result the advertising was not as effective. Potential customers need to be able to reach you. You would be surprised how many times a newspaper may transpose a number or misspell something.

Remember if you catch an error and it still goes out for public consumption that way, the newspaper will compensate you. They will usually do what they call a "make good" ad so you can recoup lost money from a bad ad. It is extremely important that whoever does the artwork uses the checklist provided. It seems like a small thing, but this checklist can save you thousands of dollars you might otherwise throw away because you missed something important in your ad.

Running a television ad

We've produced literally thousands of television ads over the years. What works in television is you have to show it and show it quickly. You will get immediate results with television so you need to run the ad when you have someone available to pick up the phone and answer that call. They won't call back again later.

We have found that advertising during certain types of shows works better than others; for example, shows like Dr. Oz and Dr. Phil work well. We have also found that shows like Wheel of Fortune and the Price is Right work well for targeting the pain and insomnia market since we are trying to reach older adults.

Remember, when you're working with your rep, they are trying to get as much money as they can from you. The process is a bit like horse-trading. Sadly, most television advertising reps assume you're never going to buy another ad so it is to their advantage to get as much money from you as they possibly can. Only twenty percent of people who buy television advertising ever want to buy it again. Your initial response to whatever deal they bring you should be no. Even if the proposal sounds good to you, say no. They have room to come down. They have automatically built in a fifty percent margin. There is wiggle room there.

When we get a proposal from a television rep, we immediately cut it in half. Then we negotiate for more discounts, which means we immediately start asking for more than what they wanted to give us. For every spot we buy during the day, we ask for another ad in the evening. Late night is when we run our insomnia ads. Those ads are generally very inexpensive. We can pay as little as $5-10 in the Bay Area for an overnight ad when we purchase a spot during the day. That will drive traffic for your insomnia program for almost nothing.

When you're creating your ad for the first time, we recommend you watch our ads and follow the directions and scripts we give you. The first thing you will need is a successful clientele to draw from. Having patients who have gotten great results makes a huge difference. That's why we constantly edit our television ads with new testimonials. We have successful clients and get them to do a short testimonial. If you do this and produce your own ad, you generally can get a fifteen percent discount. You can also have the station produce the ad when you negotiate the prices with them. They will generally do it for you for free, but you give up the fifteen percent discount. If you don't have the capacity to do it yourself, it's a great exchange. We recommend you have the station watch the example ads we have produced and let them know you want ads just like this. They should be able to accommodate your requests. You will want to make sure it's applicable to your local area. You want to look like a local business helping neighbors and friends get results in this Brain Based Wellness space.

Creating a radio ad

Radio ads are similar to TV ads except they are a lot easier to produce. Again it's the same formula when dealing with the rep. Whatever they submit to you, make sure you come back with a lower price. Have your rep work to get you extra spots, called rotators in radio. Your ads in general should be sixty-second radio ads. You never want to pay for a thirty-second radio ad. That doesn't mean you shouldn't make one however. You should always make a thirty second commercial and leave it with the station. When they need to fill thirty seconds of air time, they can reach over to the few thirty second commercials they do have and fill the air. Most radio stations have a list of different commercials they're going to pull at a specific time. We use that thirty second commercial to get bonus spots during the week.

We try to buy daytime rotation which means morning drive, mid-day, and afternoon drive. Those are the only spots we pay for. We try to get different spots in the evening for free or as a bonus. Typically we've been fortunate with our radio advertising. When we buy ten ads during the week they give us ten free ads during that same week. The only exception to this rule would be during a political season because they have what they call Political Rates and they know their ad space will fill up for that inflated price. They are not as willing to deal during these times.

They also have what they call Public Service Announcements, PSA spots. These are spots the radio station has to give away. Think about radio and TV differently from newspaper advertising. Radio and TV advertising is like a jet taking off at the airport. If a jet takes off and there are empty seats, they can't go back and fill them. So they want to put something in that space, even if it's discounted. If they don't sell that space to you at a discount, they're going to give it away to a public service announcement. Buying advertising is like anything else in life-

-if you don't ask, you don't get. You can't be afraid to ask for discounts. One of the most important tips we can give you is to always remember to tell your rep that the advertising is working okay, but it can be better. The minute you tell any of the advertising reps your business is doing great and their ads are selling great, they will never give you that discount again.

For your radio ads, we're going to give you some scripts and some example radio ads to listen to. You will be able to adapt them for your market. If you go to the station prepared with your own ad scripted or produced on your own computer, you should qualify for that fifteen percent discount. The best way to handle this is to negotiate the price for the ad first. Then you would mention that you want your fifteen percent on top of that for producing your own ads. If you ask for the fifteen percent discount before that point, they will certainly figure that into the price they give you for the advertising.

For the most part, the ads we provide with our system will be example ads. You will be able to take out our testimonial information and plugs yours in. We also have available national testimonials. As long as you're using the Mind Based Wellness, you can use those for any different area. It's okay to use those ads, but the most effective ones will be the ones that contain your local information.

Keeping the momentum

How do you keep the momentum going, and keep the patients coming in? One of our best methods is the referral cards our staff members keep with them. It contains the staff member's name, our office phone number, address and a list of what we offer in our office. On the backside of the card, it has a fifteen percent off offer and we have our staff sign their name on it. Our staff gets a five percent referral fee for anyone that comes in and signs up with that card. It's a great incentive to have them handing them out to everyone they can, and we're also handing them out at talks and events as well, whenever we can. If we go to a social event, then they get our business card and on the back of the card there's always a referral or something free for them to get them into the clinic. It gives us a good opportunity to talk to them about what we do. It gives them a reason to take action and come to the clinic.

Emails are going to be another important avenue for you to tap into. If you don't have an email list at this time, we recommend you start building one. We are committed to putting together content to build email campaigns. Email is free and can be an extremely effective marketing tool. We've found sending out a weekly newsletter is great. We also send out a monthly newsletter in regular mail; so every week they get a quick email update and every month they get a physical newsletter. We include a calendar of events to keep people aware of when they can come to the clinic and when we are hosting seminars and events they may be interested in. This is a simple way to keep your business in the forefront of clients' minds.

We are also going to provide you with samples of our mail-out letters. We usually do three different offers in our mailings. The first one was three sessions with fifty percent off. This mailing usually goes out in June and would go out to clients who were already in the program and were interested in continuing but perhaps didn't for monetary reasons. They will also be able to give the referral card to all of their family and friends.

In July we send out our two-for-one offer. This is to target those clients who may have been interested in the June offer, but didn't have three people to do that particular offer with. Almost everyone can find at least one person that might be interested in the program with them. This is a simple way to keep cash flow up during the leaner summer months.

Our last mailing of the summer is in August. This is a thirty five percent off for one person. This will target those people who, for one reason or another, didn't have anyone else to sign up with them. August is a notoriously slow month, one of the slowest of the year. This mailer enables us to keep the same cash flow coming into the practice during our slowest month.

Remember, publicity is important. You want to be an active

publicist for your own company. Use caution though. Ask for details when you're asked to do news stories, because unfortunately oftentimes they are looking for a negative story. You want to make sure it's a positive story. We tend to invite the journalist in and then we bring in successful patients to speak about their experiences. In fact, even in times where we may not have time to do an interview ourselves, we would still arrange for patients to come and speak to the journalist and give them information about their experiences. When you're talking to them, keep it simple. Avoid jargon and give them something newsworthy, something that's going on in your practice. This helps you get the results you want from this story.

We also have a physician referral program we'll make available to you. People can be unaware of how valuable a tool this is. Many people believe physicians wouldn't be interested in referring their patients to a chiropractic clinic and they may be right; but when presented in the context of the Brain Based Wellness program you would be surprised how many physicians will absolutely refer their patients in for that. So we ask our patients, is it okay for us to keep your physician informed of your result? Then we write a letter to the doctor and on the envelope it would say, "Confidential Patient Information." That means the doctor is obligated to open the letter and read it. This is not a marketing letter. We just inform them that their patient has started our program, that we have a guarantee and general information. This is our first letter. The second letter is all about her results. Even if she's not getting the results, we send a letter to the doctor saying, "Just want to let you know Betty is at a standing point now. She hasn't lost the 1-3 pounds a week which is normal in our program, but we are going to keep with her. To date, she has taken off fifteen pounds of her forty pound goal."

Every time you send out a letter they have to open it, read it and put it in the patient file. When the patient comes back to see the physician they are going to talk to the doctor about your program. The doctor is used to referring patients out, so when they see someone with an issue such as weight loss they will remember your client and say, "I don't do anything with weight loss but they have this clinic down the road. They can help you with weight loss or stopping smoking or stress reduction or whatever the issue is."

Along with sending physicians letters, we also invite local physicians from our area to attend any of our client events. We want them to come and see we're not just the average run-of-the-mill chiropractor or weight loss clinic. We use the latest scientific techniques and are using the Brain Based Wellness solutions. We want them to come in and experience it. We've found that being up-front and communicating with physicians is the best way to build our business in this way. Our clinic in Virginia Beach actually had 72 referring physicians. By that point we could have spent nothing in advertising and still had a successful business just through those referrals

Another simple advertising method is making sure you have a results based environment. Any testimonial you get, put it in a binder at the front of the clinic for everyone to see. Start taking videos of successful patients to play in your lobby while patients wait. We will give you more information regarding these processes when you go through the entire Brain Based Wellness training.

Mistakes and how to avoid them

The first mistake doctors make is lack of communication with the patient. You need to learn to be able to embody this. It's the main thing most doctors miss. The most successful doctors with this system are those who can communicate effectively with their patients.
The know-it-all patient is a problem because they think they need to know everything about the program before they can start using it. Nothing could be further from the truth. Dr. Richard Bandler, the co-founder of NLP says, "Anything worth doing well is worth doing poorly at first." You have to be willing to adapt, improvise, and overcome those obstacles and you have to start somewhere.

When we talk about closing the sale with a patient, a lot of doctors are afraid to ask for the money. Remember, you can always go down in price, but you can't go up. Figure out what you need to make, double it, ask for it, and you're going to be amazed at how many people will pay it. Then if you have to give them a discount, like the doctor we talked about earlier, you have the room in your profit margin to do it.

When your staff answers the telephone, you want to take charge. You want to get them in the door without answering too many questions in depth and we never quote a price on the phone. It's important to move the potential patient to an office environment. Once you get them into the office they will see all the posters and brochures that make up the success environment. You can focus them on results and give them a free demonstration of what you have available.

Let the product, the Brain Based Wellness solution, the MindFit, do the selling for you. If you try to explain everything on the phone, it will put people off. They get bombarded with information and it's too much for them to process at one time. If you confuse them too quickly, they are not going to take action. We want to help them to take the action step, come on in, try it out, and then we're going to have one of our staff go over the benefits of the program for you once you've experienced it. It's a simple sale.

When you think about the seven steps to an effective sale, you can easily compare it to a chiropractic exam. You identify the pain, overcome the misconceptions, explain the program and how it works, answer any questions, explain fees, schedule the appointment and get the payment.

During the sales process you should act as if they've already bought. Most salespeople who are highly effective don't ask if they're going to buy. They simply ask them when they want to make their first appointment. You want to take the choice right off the table. Convince them that you're evaluating to see if they are a good candidate for your program and once you do, you suggest the right program and get them started.

Why People Don't Buy

It is important for you to understand the four reasons people don't buy a program from you. It boils down to what we call CATS. C stands for commitment. You have to remember they're not committed to you. The most important thing is to get them committed to you and the program at some level.

A stands for affordable. We always say we're not going to let money stand between someone and their happiness. Work out the payments for them. They can do it.

T stands for time. Most people don't think they have the time to do the program. So they have to have the ability to spend time to get the results or they're not going to happen.

S stands for spouse. You have to get agreement from the spouse and make sure they're onboard with the program as well or you could be dealing with a sabotage situation and the patient won't see results. As you're evaluating this potential patient, if these four issues are not dealt with, they are not going to see optimal results. It's important that you address each of these points if they come up and get rid of the CATS to get down to the sale.

Assignment

If you're going to do some outside advertising--whether it be radio, TV or paid ads in the local paper--you will need to set up meetings with your media reps. Enlist successful patients to share testimonials. Video testimonials are great because it allows people to see the real person, hear the tone, see facial expressions. It's best to be able to get both a written and video testimonial from successful patients.

Make a commitment to speak in the community at least twice a month. Get yourself invited to events and don't be afraid to speak about this program. In some cases it's been difficult to speak on chiropractic. Remember, now you're speaking about a wide variety of things including natural weight loss, overcoming stress and making stress work for you. You're speaking on topics like curing insomnia. These are topics people will gladly have you speak about. Print up your flyers and distribute them at these events, including the free session offer.

We like to set people up with a free demo whenever possible, giving them a chance to test it out for fifteen or twenty minutes. They will find they are more relaxed, peaceful and calm and it's easy to convince them to want to use this on an ongoing basis. Don't forget to take the time to use the technology yourself each and every day, working on the things that matter to you.

There has been a lot of information covered in this book, but it all has been tested and proven to help you succeed and achieve your goals in implementing your own program in your clinic. Everything we have shared with you is practical, time-tested and it works absolutely everywhere and every time. If you need further explanation on anything you have read in here, please do not hesitate to contact Patrick at drpositive@gmail.com or Bob at bob@themasterscircle.com. We want you to succeed with this program and will help in any way we can. You can ask us any questions you might have and we'd certainly love for you to share your victories.

This is a community project. We want everyone to win and we want everyone to profit. This has been a treasure trove of information. If you just follow the program, follow the steps we've given you, we believe you will be successful. Many doctors in this program are doing exactly that, and reaping the rewards. We want that for all of you as well.

We want to thank you for growing with us, thank you for thinking outside of the box and being willing to make the changes necessary for phenomenal growth and sustainability.

CHAPTER
NINE

Implementation –
Your Key to Lasting Results

Implementation – Your key to lasting results

In this chapter we're going to explain the different methods for implementation that are available to you. There is no limit to what you can do to implement Brain Based Wellness programs in your clinic. The only limit is your own imagination. We are going to suggest some of the more common ways, the easiest ways to implement, but feel free to be creative. Remember, if what you're offering is with the patient's best interest at heart, you cannot fail. If what you're offering also happens to be highly profitable to you, it's icing on the cake. We want you to be as excited as we are about this cutting edge technology. These implementation strategies should help you figure out what is going to work best in your environment, within the office space you currently have. As you move forward, you'll have the opportunity to branch out as you learn what is working in other offices and come up with new ideas on your own. Just start maximizing the results with your patients first and then let the money follow. Using a simple example, if you could use Brain Based Wellness to add just five patients a day and charge an average price of $50 per session, that adds up to around $50,000 a year that you weren't maximizing on previously.

Remember, though, we are not really trying to sell individual sessions. We're selling the whole package in order to best rewire the patient's brain, and create new synaptic connections that will create a balance between the sympathetic and the parasympathetic nervous system; allowing the brain to reset, re-boot, re-harmonize, heal, and work more efficiently. These things take repetition and time. In our experience, we have found that at least two sessions per week is ideal for most patients over a twelve-week time period.

It's important to understand it's just as easy to sell someone one session as it is to sell them a full program. Think of it in terms of chiropractic adjustments. You could sell a patient one adjustment but then each time they come in, you have to continually resell them to come in for the next adjustment. It makes more sense to sell a care plan. The same applies to the Brain Based Wellness program. As we demonstrated in a previous chapter, you should sell from the top down, starting with your ultimate package. In our center, we have a weight-loss program called the Ultimate Body Contouring Package.

Our goal is to try to sell this program first and work down. You can always go lower in price, but it's very difficult to go up in price.

Most potential patients are going to want the best and they are looking to you as their doctor to tell them what the best program is for them. When you think about what your office offers, you don't have to have the Neuropathy and Lipo Lights. You don't have to have the Infrared Saunas. All of those things are extra. When we first started out, all we had was a small office space. We out grew that office within six weeks. In our first year we had to move three times to accommodate the clientele. We're not recommending that for you. We want you to be bursting at the seams before you think about moving, or building out another room in your office. Don't get carried away too early.

Packages

You're already aware of the top five programs that we offer-- weight loss, stress management, overcoming chronic pain, preventing or eliminating insomnia and smoking cessation. We can't stress enough that these are not the only programs. They are only a small selection of what we have available. We also offer other programs that while not as popular in number of clients, have proven just as valuable such as winning relationships, accelerated learning, self-mastery, menopause, wealth accumulation and vibrant health. These are easy to sell to the people who are looking for those specific skills right now. Again it's completely up to the individual doctor to decide which programs they want to run, but based on our experience the condition-based programs are the best sellers

It's also important to listen to your patient because they are going to tell you within the evaluative process which issue they're really looking for help with. Most times there will be a Brain Based Wellness component to it and then you are free to add in whatever other components you feel they need from a physician's standpoint.

Frequency

We've been asked a lot about the frequency with which the program should be applied. In our experience we have found that the best frequency for most patients is two MindFit sessions a week. Two visits a week is the most economical and practical way for an average patient to participate in the program and make significant continuous progress, all the while keeping the price affordable. The MindFit equipment has a cumulative effect. If you can use the equipment at an average of every seventy-two hours, it starts to retrain the brain, gets those neurons wiring and firing together around the idea of health, harmony and vitality in the body. For you, the doctor, and your staff it's ideal to do the program every day or, at the least, four or five times per week. The more frequently you do it, the better results you're going to have.

The main goal here is to create a habit of success because what your patients have been experiencing in the past is a pattern of failure. They have to be committed to their own healing, and we have found once they get started on this program, that's not an issue. We have also made a point of keeping connected with our patients. So if we find they are coming in twice a week, what we do is we call them in between visits just to get a little update to see how they're doing, to see if they're following along with their prescribed program. We know it's easy to fall back into old patterns, especially for the first few weeks, and taking this extra step adds accountability and also adds that personal touch that so many patients are looking for.

If for some reason you are not able to get them in the door twice a week, then you would assign them homework. In NLP or Neuro-Linguistic Programming, we call this, "Task View." If they don't have the MindFit at home, or they don't have the equipment they need, then we might give them this homework to do before they go to bed at night. They go to bed ten minutes earlier just to review and go over the successes they have had during the day. It's important to stress the successes of the day because most people go to sleep, unfortunately, dwelling on all their failures. We want to get them into the habit of success. As they start seeing results, many patients will be interested in buying the equipment for use at home. Eighty-five percent of the patients coming through our centers will buy a MindFit for home care either during their program or after it is complete.

Week One

We consider week one of each patient's program a clearing session. This is the week that trains the brain to clear out negative clutter and self-talk, and moves them through the program by beginning to build new resources and skills. Each program builds on the one before it, so it's extremely important to take them in order. When you're working on a specific issue you should start with week one and move through the program so you get the benefit of going through the training the way it was designed to be used. We always call it success by the numbers. Follow those numbers and succeed.

We've already said it, but we can't stress enough how important it is for you as the doctor to be doing these programs yourself on a regular basis. This is how we show the best versions of ourselves. This is how we heal, and this is how we allow the healing to take place from the top down and from inside out. It's also how we give our patients the best results. This is how we have the most confidence and the most energy. This is how we communicate more effectively. I cannot stress enough the doctor has got to heal him or herself before they can be healing their practice and their patients.

Getting people through the door

A big question we get asked a lot is how do you get people in? Well the best offer ever is FREE. We've been through this before but we're just going to go over a refresher on some free ways to market your business.

The first and best thing you can do is ask current successful patients for referrals. When patients are doing well we give them referral cards. They put their name on them and hand them out to family and friends. When a referred person turns one of the referral cards in to us, we will give the patient a referral bonus. This usually entails shopping for supplements at our center or going towards a discount on a MindFit or even extending their program by a month for each referral that comes in. Referral cards are a powerful tool. The patient has already done the groundwork for you. If they weren't being successful they wouldn't refer the program to someone else, so you know they've already raved about you. It's not a hard sell.

When you advertise you should offer something for free. They can come in to a free seminar. They can have an introductory ride on the MindFit. Whatever you need to do to get them in the door, because once they're in the door, they can see who you are and what you offer and they are going to want to be part of your system. The wording we'd use in this type of advertising runs along these lines. "We are so convinced that our system will help you that we'd like you to experience it for free." Once they have the experience, there's a shift and it's not hard to convince them they need what you have.

For example, we have had people come into our clinic for insomnia. We challenged them to do a ten minute session, come back the next day and tell us how they felt. They both came back and purchased the MindFit because they had the best night's sleep they'd had in years, just from a ten-minute refresher. Most people are going to experience a significant shift in their physical being because their energy has been replenished and their mind now functions better and they are going to want more of that feeling.

Another option for marketing the MindFit system is to have someone utilizing it in your reception area. This is not the ideal situation, but it has worked for several doctors who had small offices. They soon discovered there was a side-benefit.

People will come into your clinic and natural curiosity will take over. They'll ask, What's that person doing? This creates a perfect opening for your staff to explain the Brain Based Wellness addition to your office and generating awareness and interest in current patients trying this out. Noise canceling headphones are recommended for lobby sessions.

Advertising

If you've already come on board with our Brain Based Wellness program and are interested in reviewing the advertising we've been talking about in previous chapters, you will need to go to your log in page for www.selfmasterytechnology.com. Once you're logged in, there is a button that says "doctors log-in." Click that and find the link that says "Advertising Downloads." Once you have that downloaded, you can watch our TV advertising and you can listen to the radio advertising. The scripts for those are also available for download at this location, giving you a template to utilize with your own, local information.

Also at this location we will have newspaper ads for your use as well as direct marketing tools and examples. You will notice that on every direct mail marketing piece we have utilized in the past, they all have one thing in common. They offer a free session. What this means is after they come in for the free evaluation session, we allow them to experience a free session. In the chiropractic world it would be similar to giving a free report of findings and then moving on to explaining what program will work best for them.

Best practices

Below you'll find outlined what we consider best practices of our most successful centers. We highly recommend you utilize as many of these practices in your own location.

First--Every center that is getting phenomenal results with this program is using the demo session all the time. This means when you have a patient come in the door, whether they are new or existing, explain to them you have this new, amazing technology called Brain Based Wellness that you're giving them the opportunity to try for free. Tell them they're going to be listening to Dr. Patrick Porter, who will explain about this program and how it works. Put them in the earphones and glasses and let the demo do the selling work.

Second--When you're online at the site you will find a link to produce our flyers at cost from Vista Print. Once you have those it is easy to promote this system in-house. Each successful practice that is part of our network does this. There are six different promotional pieces, which means you have six weeks of promotion. After six weeks you rotate back to the first one. These have been tested and proven to be the top six producers out there.

Third--Our most successful locations offer seminars. These can be done in-house or out of the office. As an example, one of our doctors invited a group of patients that he knew wanted to lose weight to a special presentation to launch his new twelve-week all natural weight loss program. He offered this at no cost or obligation. He allowed them to invite whoever they wanted to attend with them capping the maximum at fifty people. He had fifty people show up to his seminar, all interested in losing weight. He promoted his twelve week program, sticking to the four basic points that we emphasize: This program is doctor supervised, it is all natural, there is no diet or deprivation and that he would be utilizing the latest technology to balance the brain to end emotional eating once and for all. He told them they should expect to lose one to three pounds a week over the twelve-week period. He would be offering classes that were optional on health and nutrition.

He emphasized to this group that they would be his first test group and offered them a reduced price of $1500 if they pre-paid for their entire program. He signed up thirty-eight patients that night and after the fifth week of the program his patients had already cumulatively lost 425 pounds.

The point of that story is, if someone else can do it, you can follow that model and do it just as well and even better. In weight loss, for example, we find that the most successful doctors give weight loss sales presentations in the same way you would think about your chiropractic report of findings. They have a problem. You have a solution. You have to figure out if they have the problems we can help with, and in most cases we can. There have been very few occasions over the years where we've had to turn people away. That's the reason for the evaluation process. You have to make sure they are a good fit for your program and they're going to be compliant with what you're offering.

Enrolling and closing

When you think about enrolling someone into a program, your mindset should be that every person coming into your office needs what you're offering. That's also the way you think about chiropractic care. It's not about pain anymore. It's about wellness and it's about making people healthy. The same is true with Brain Based Wellness.

If you're not comfortable with selling, be sure you have the right salesperson staffed in your office. We have seen some people that are not great at selling the program, but had no problem asking for the money. We've also seen people who could give a great sales presentation but in the end could not bring themselves to ask for the money. If the latter is you, you need to practice standing in front of the mirror repeating to yourself, it's only $2000, or it's only $3000, whatever the amount may be. Work at this until it is effortless for you. There's no stress in the words.

Once you' have delivered that line, stop. Let the person process, and don't second-guess what he or she is thinking. What we've found is during that time they're usually trying to figure out how they can pay. Let them come up with a solution, even if it takes two or three minutes. You don't want to let them sit there forever without saying anything. Eventually you can give them a nudge with something like, "Do you want me to help you out a little bit with how you can pay for this?" That's the time to tell them about the payment options that are available. Remember you're a professional. You deserve a professional fee. We don't recommend offering discounts just to get the sale done. You're worth every penny you're asking for.

The other thing we like to do is once someone makes the commitment, schedule the first appointment and collect the money then. Every doctor should be able to do this. We say it like this. "We know that you're an excellent candidate for our program. I'm going to recommend that you start out with our twelve-week program here. Let's get started on Monday. In many instances this is where the real selling takes place, when they say no, but many times, they never say no. They just go along and enroll in the program because you've explained it well enough to them. They understand this is doctor-supervised program and that you're going to get them the results. Then you collect the money from them or you have a designated staff member do it. Many doctors are more comfortable with that option.

Going back to the earlier top down theory of sales, you need to have a deluxe Cadillac program and then at least one other program to offer them. This comes down to the power of perception. Dr. Chaldini from Arizona State University had a story to illustrate this. He was on campus at ASU when he was approached by two boy scouts asking if he would be interested in sponsoring their scout troop to go to the jamboree. He didn't have children and wasn't particularly interested. The boys said, "Well, if you aren't interested in sponsoring us, would you at least be interested in buying a couple chocolate bars?" When the kids left, he was standing there with two chocolate bars, despite the fact that he doesn't like chocolate. He bought the chocolate bars because it was a better option for him than the sponsorship and he wanted to help these two kids. The same thing is true with your patients. They want to please you, but sometimes they just can't say yes to the first thing; but maybe they'll say yes to the second thing. That's selling from the top down.

This is also called present and retreat, but you have to have something to retreat to. If you only have one program, you're going to get a yes or no. We like to ask them, "Would you prefer this program or that one?" That alleviates the yes or no response.

It's important in the sale to do pre-framing, which means presenting the information as if the client has already purchased. It's not when you decide or when you sign up. Present the information within the framework of when you come in or when you do your sessions. Put into their mind's eye the framework in which you want them to analyze the information they're getting.

Make sure you explain the guarantee, if you have one, remembering we don't guarantee results. We guarantee our education. Make sure you explain how the guarantee works. In our case, we have the guarantee that says at the end of our program, if you feel like you didn't get what you needed during our program, you can continue to come in twice a month at no charge. The guarantee is offered to take the risk out of the buy for the patient in the first place.

We always recommend if you're having trouble signing people up or enrolling them, record your conversations. Listen to what you are saying and find out what pictures you're creating with the words you are choosing to use. Your words are creating pictures and images in your prospects' minds that are either helping them to make the decision to be a part of your program or repelling them from the program. You want to make sure you're using the right words to create the pictures that create success.

When you're giving a potential patient a free session, you should use wording like, "There is this amazing new technology out that helps to balance our brain and relax us and allow our bodies to heal. I'd like you to try it for ten or twenty minutes--depending on which program you choose--if you're a good candidate, you are either going to fall asleep, or at the end you're going to be relaxed, centered, and peaceful. If you have any of these types of results, it's a positive test and you will thrive with a twelve week program. Then put them on the demo.

Because we have been doing this for years, we know in advance that ninety-nine out of one hundred people are going to come out and rave about how amazing this is. Then, because you pre-framed them, you can then sit down and say, "Great! That's the result I was expecting. I'm thrilled that you got that. Now, as I said before the demo, if you get a positive test, it is an indicator that you will thrive in this program and allow yourself to heal at the highest level. Let's go over how the program works."

Bullet proof evaluation

Over the years we have developed what we like to call the "Bullet Proof Evaluation." What this entails is a check list of sorts, much like ones used by pilots before takeoff. The important thing is to remember to start each evaluation fresh, regardless of what happened with the last patient you saw or the telephone call you just received.

Leave your luggage at the door. People will notice the difference when you are presenting if you are totally with them versus when you are distracted. Just be present in the evaluation.

Another good tip is not to sell expecting the objections. That's a mistake many new evaluators make. Go in with the mindset that everyone is going to buy and only handle objections when and if they come up. If you start trying to handle objections before they even show their face you run the risk of putting them in the patient's mind when they may never have even thought of it on their own. Keep it simple. Be clear and precise in your explanations. We've spent years trying to simplify the complex ways of doing things. Your sales process should be so simple a child could understand it.

Remember, when we are speaking or communicating with someone, it's important to understand we are speaking to their subconscious which is no more educated than a 4th grader. Even though you might have a college PhD or be a doctor, the reality is that the part of the mind we really need to reach is the subconscious. You have to learn to speak to that part of their mind in a way that is not insulting and is clear and precise.

Avoid going into sales pitch mode which means you have a script and you follow this script no matter who is sitting across from you. Each patient is unique. If you have fourteen different patients you should see fourteen different ways to explain the same program to them to make it relevant to that particular person. We're going to use their life, their criteria, the information we've drawn from. As Steven Covey says, "You must understand before you can be understood." So we have to understand where they are at before we can get them to understand where we are at. If we start explaining into a space that's not relevant to them, we will break rapport. Maintain eye contact as much as possible without staring them down. Some people won't buy from you if you don't look them in the eye because it conveys a lack of confidence about the subject you're talking about.

Use newscasters as an example. If you've ever watched a newscaster at work, they don't bob their head. They look sincerely straight into the camera and tell the facts. You need to present your program in much the same way. You need to be confident and reassuring. The confidence and energy you portray is going to ultimately be what sells them, not the actual words you use. Words are empowering but it's all in the delivery. What are you bringing to the experience? Are you present with them? Are you confident with it? Are you sure of yourself?

When we say, Lead, don't sell," what we mean by that is lead them to the decision because they need to make the decision. When we're doing an evaluation, the best result you can get is when they say back to you things like: This is the program I need. I need to balance my brain. I need to get rid of the emotional eating. I need to know how to handle my stress.

You need to make sure that you get to that point in the conversation before you ever ask for a dollar. Once they start selling you on those ideas, then you know you've done a good job. Then you can easily ask for the money.

Now, if they choose not to enroll, then what you want to do is make sure you set up the next contact. You can schedule them for a return visit with their spouse or schedule a time to talk on the telephone. You can schedule them to attend one of your free demos or a welcome class. In our centers, we hold a welcome class twice a week. We also send a handwritten note to each person we evaluate. We have had many, many clients return to our center and sign up simply because we sent them a personalized thank you note.

If you find that you are not the sales person for your office, we often find that it works to promote in house staff. Your front desk administrator or a CA is usually the best candidate for this because they already know all there is to know about the programs. If you choose to hire a sales professional, generally we start them off part time, advising them to keep whatever job they currently have, until we see how they work out, but we have had great success hiring this way. You never know where the next great sales person could be hiding.

Exiting the program

In this section we're going to discuss best practices for when patients complete their programs. In our clinic, we have every patient go through what we call an "exit interview." We want to ensure during this interview that we have kept all our commitments. We want to know that we have delivered on whatever we said we were going to do for this particular patient. This is a good check-in system, because one of the most powerful tools at your disposal is word of mouth or referrals. Someone who got good results in your program will tell three people and refer them to your clinic. If they're not happy, however, they're going to tell everyone they can think of, adversely affecting potential future patients.

Exit interviews offer us three important things. First, we make sure the patient feels they got all the service they needed. Second, it provides us an opportunity to offer them any additional services they need or desire. The third is to obtain a testimonial from another happy patient. We prefer to get video testimonials if possible. They are great for your reception area where prospective patients are waiting. It gives a real person to attach the problem to. People read these true stories and think, This person had the same problem I have and they did it. Maybe I can do it, too.

Your job is to make sure they are raving fans of the job you did for them. One way to accomplish this is to communicate with them at the end of their program. You might ask them something like, Tell me a little bit about how the program worked for you. I see here you've lost twelve pounds--or you're sleeping through the night consistently--or you've stopped smoking--or whatever goal they wanted to accomplish. There should be some documentation there. If everything is going well and they're ready to move on, then the next question should be around after care. Simply ask, What have you planned for home care?

At this point, explain to the patient that they have invested three months' time and money into retraining their brain and you want to make sure they will be successful for the rest of their lives, so they need to have a plan. Usually the patient doesn't plan, and we all know what happens at that point. If you don't plan to succeed, you're certain to fail. We want to set them up for success.

As we stated before, about eighty five percent of our patients buy a MindFit machine. Fifty percent of them do it at that meeting when we're planning the future with them. If they feel that's not an option for them, we also offer them continued visits on a per session basis.

We usually charge $85 a month for a maintenance program, pointing out at the same time that taking home a MindFit only costs $395, the cost of around four months payments and we're going to give you 16 sessions with the package. If they want to add more sessions later it's very simple to go online and purchase as many as they want. That's when most people go ahead and buy that program. Our patients don't even know it's available to buy until after the third week that they're in the program. We don't want them to focus on anything else but coming into the clinic and getting into the habit of success. Once we feel they have embodied that principle, we mention that it's available for home use as well.

Don't be concerned with trying to upsell your patients with this technology. Some doctors do have issue with this. They feel like the patient has already paid and they are not comfortable selling them something else. Remember, you're doing them a service. When someone owns this equipment and uses it regularly, they are going to get much better results than someone who only has the opportunity to use it twice a week. They're getting the expertise of the doctor and they're getting the clinical experience, and hopefully you're also adding into the chiropractic adjustment. This technology at home is a bonus. Of course they can't give themselves their own chiropractic adjustment at home and they can't get the coaching at home; so this is a way to add a new revenue stream to your practice with the primary goal of giving them long-term success.

Oftentimes, we find we have done such a good job motivating and improving a patient's life that they will enter a new program when they finish their first program. Twenty five percent of the time in our centers we have found that they will upgrade to an entirely different program or enter into the continuity program at $85 a month. During the exit interview is a great time to bring this issue up. You should review their initial paperwork to see if they brought up any collateral issues that they wanted to work on in addition to the primary issue. For example, they came to us to stop smoking but now they want to lose weight. Quite often we will give them a discount of twenty five percent on the new program. If they decide not to opt for a new program, then you can just say, "Well, you know what? We will be here when you are ready to take that next step." And leave it at that. You've opened the door and you just need to wait for them to walk back through it.

Assignment

We want you to set a daily, weekly and monthly goal. How many packages are you going to sell if you sell one a day in your office 4 days a week and that sale is approximately $4000 worth of income per week? What are your objectives? If you're going to do a twelve-week weight loss program as we've discussed earlier, is your goal to sign up ten, fifteen or fifty people? You need to have a goal. If you don't have a target, it's impossible to hit it.

Recognize that a very important key to this entire program is that it is staff run. The whole idea is to expand the scope of your practice in ways that keeps you earning money even when you don't have your hands on a patient. For this reason, you need to ensure you're hiring the right people, training them correctly and rewarding them properly. Evaluate your current staff and put a plan in place with targets or milestones for hiring. How many people do you need? How many full-time? How many part-time? This will grow and change and evolve over time as you get deeper and deeper into the engagement of this process Richard Bandler, the renowned co-founder of Neuro-Linguistic Programming once said, "Anything worth doing well is worth doing terribly at first." You have to have everything in place to start implementing. It's okay to implement with what you have and know you can always improve on it because whatever you do, by following the procedures we've outlined for you here, you're going to increase the results you're seeing in your clinic and increase your bottom line.

CHAPTER
TEN

**What the experts have to say about
Brain Based Wellness**

What the experts have to
say about Brain-Based Wellness

Q and A with Jared Leon, DC

Why is brain-based adjusting so important, and a major step forward in the transformation of chiropractic?

The aim and purpose of brain-based adjusting is to create a true functional integration of the brain. The whole concept of chiropractic, which goes all the way back to D.D. Palmer is to fix and help balance tone. The reality is, if we give muscular tone to the body, through a chiropractic adjustment, the goal is to send a message to the spinal nerve through the spinal cord to the contralateral brain. If that doesn't equate well, if it's on the wrong side, the higher functioning side, which is referred to as the increased frequency or firing side, we're going to turn that side of the brain up even higher, making the balance and function worse. The physiological changes for the patient are not going to be optimal. Theoretically, you could end up making the patient worse on a physiological scale.

The main reason brain-based functionality is so important to balance our brain is because the most important job we have as a chiropractor is to optimize the nervous system, and the actual output of how the brain functions. By adjusting the appropriate side of the body, to increase the deficit or decrease the brain, we're going to optimize the balance of the brain, cortex-for-cortex, hemisphere-for-hemisphere. We are, therefore, optimizing the physiology and all of the brain processes going forward.

Unilateral adjusting creates bilateral brain balance on the appropriate side.

Can you give us a few practical ways to analyze brain imbalance, and explain what those findings mean?

There are three or four indicators I always look for first. Again the whole goal of the chiropractic adjustment is to gain central integration, to do that we want to start with the eyes because that's where most of the brain functionality is going to occur. Dr. Richard Barwell says the eyes are an extension of the brain.

When people have two symmetrical eyes, we know they have good brain function. So we're looking for a deficit in the eyes; for one eye to be more closed which would be a cranial nerve three, four or five deficit, which we know is a sign of a hyperactive opposite cortex. We then compare the one pupil to the other, and if there is a marked size difference between the two, it again means something is imbalanced in the brain.

For a balanced brain, we're looking for balanced pupils. It's important to know the largest pupil is going to be on the opposite side to the one that's imbalanced. In other words, you're going to need to adjust the side with the smallest pupil, as this is the side that is imbalanced.

The next indicator we need to look for is called pyramidal weakness. This involves getting the patient to hold their arms and hands out straight in front of them and hold their fingers tightly together; we then need to get them to resist as we push down on their hands to test their extensor muscles. If the brain is equal and in balance, it should equate to equal hand strength, grip strength and extensor strength.

When we have someone come in with an increased frequency of firing in the brain on one side, and a decrease on the other, it works like a seesaw. When one goes up, the other must come down. When doing the test, if the brain is imbalanced, you will see you will be able to push one hand substantially easier than the other; it will be unbelievably weaker.

This means you will need to adjust the opposite side to the one that is the weakest because the brain works in opposites. So if you found, for example, the right side was considerably weaker than the left, you will need to adjust the left side to bring the brain into balance. Another indicator of this imbalance is looking for increased rashes or vascularity issues on one side of the body more than the other; this is a good indicator, especially in children. So if you have rashes that occur on one side, or you have acne on one side or just a random spot, it is usually a sign of the same thing.

You will always see the pyramidal weakness, the increased pupil, and the rashes all on the same side. On children this is a major indicator, especially babies because you can't do a pyramidal pathway on a baby. Therefore, this combination is a great indicator to let you know the baby's brain is imbalanced, and to guide you as to which side you need to work on.

Another good indicator is if the side you're adjusting has an internal rotation of the upper extremity on postural exams. So on the upper extremity, they are going to have an increased internal rotation of the upper arm on the side you're going to have to adjust, opposite the pyramidal path. You'll also find an external rotation of the foot on the same side. The whole leg is going to be external and the arm is going to be internal. You can then correlate that with the muscular imbalances. This is also where you're going to find they have all of their pain.

All of the low back pain they may be experiencing is going to be on the opposite pyramidal path, along with the upper arm pain, and pains in the chest, biceps and forearm. So that's going to be a great indicator as well.

When you document a brain imbalance, which is producing vertebral subluxation, how do you adjust it unilaterally to create hemispheric balance?

Say for example C5 is subluxated; we're not going to use the old paradigm of trying to move the prominent area back towards the middle. What we're doing is adjusting the opposite side of the brain imbalance by using an instrument or just your hand on the vertebra that is subluxated.

So if you know you need to focus on one side, it allows you to be the true artist in the chiropractic format. It takes creativity and allows you to think through the three-dimensionality of every bone, to allow for the stimulation of the right neurology.

In other words, even if there is a subluxation in one area, we're going to note it and take care of every other subluxation we find on the appropriate side. Then when we're done, we're going to recheck the subluxation we left and we should find it is corrected based on proper brain tone.

You have to be more creative and more functional because you're going to find the central integrations will end up being much greater for the patient. So much so that if you have a muscle spasm, for example, it could be gone in seconds, or even nano seconds, as long as you're on the appropriate side of the brain. But subluxation is there based on a compensation of the brain, so it's there on purpose to save some function of the brain that we could be hurting.

You need to be adjusting the one side of the body specifically using your hand or an instrument to put it back into a normal position to allow the mechanical receptors to function at their best. After you have done the adjustment, as they're walking, talking and moving in life, they're stimulating the neurological health of the opposite brain. They're going to start to feel incredible, and as the day goes on, they're going to be feeling better and better.

Simply put, by adjusting the appropriate side of the brain imbalance, we're able to transform our thinking from adjusting to relieve interference—to adjusting to stimulate and optimize the hemispheric balance of the brain.

It's a transformation in chiropractic philosophy if you will, a new paradigm. We're adjusting our patients not because we want to move a bone from point A to point B, but because we're trying to stimulate brain balance.

We're using the patient's spine almost as a lever system. If a lever goes one way and it goes off-balance we need to bring it back into balance. We're using the adjustment of the spine to stimulate the opposite brain so your patient will have brain balance when they leave the office. They're going to feel like they've never felt before, because even if their joints are in alignment, if we don't stimulate the right side of the brain, they're not going to have central integration.

We're not just trying to relieve nerve pressure anymore. That will be one of the end results, but we've moved onto a higher purpose, which is to create brain integration and balance.

What additional and practical ways are there to help create balance and integration, in addition to the adjustment?

In addition to the adjustment, you can utilize a tuning fork at 128 Hz on the same side that you've just adjusted. We want to increase brain function as much as we can, and the vibrations from the tuning fork will take the same path through the spinal nerve to the spinal cord to the opposite brain. This way we're able to maximize brain function, but we don't have to adjust as much as we would normally have to do. By using the tuning fork, we are able to slowly drip the information in at a much slower rate, which is great for children and people with Autism and ADHD. If you over-stimulate the brain too quickly, you can end up having a negative spillover effect and the patient can end up feeling worse.

Another great technique we use is to occlude one nostril. Again, it's going to be on the side we will be adjusting because we want it to have an effect on the opposite side of the brain. We're going to occlude one nostril and then allow the patient to smell an essential oil such as peppermint, lavender or eucalyptus for around two or three breaths. This way we're able to bypass the spinal nerve roots and go directly to the brain functionality using the cranial nerve. We're stimulating the brain on a specific level; for some patients this may be the only treatment they can use. With people who have fibromyalgia, for example, their spine is already over-stimulated and they may not be able to tolerate any of the other methods we have been discussing.

Thoughts on Brain-Based Wellness
from Richard Barwell, DC

I practiced as a strict chiropractic clinician for thirty-two years before I started to look further into what chiropractic adjustments were really doing. I can tell you, when I did start thinking about it, it changed my life. I started working with some of the pioneers in the field of neurofeedback and this is what ultimately led to the development of neurologically-based chiropractic—the concept of revisiting chiropractic from its original roots. It also led to the development of the NeuroInfiniti. The Neuroinfiniti helps us to see the effect of the chiropractic adjustment on the neurological functions of the brain.

The signature move of the chiropractor is the chiropractic adjustment. What is it about the adjustment that makes chiropractic get such consistently great results?

When we started doing brainwave testing, we were able to see the amazing difference between the pre- and post chiropractic adjustments and the incredible power a chiropractic adjustment has to alter the central nervous system functions.

When we gathered pre- and post-EEG studie,s we saw massive changes in neurological function, and we came to realize the adjustments we were doing were a huge neurological pattern interrupt.
Can you clarify what you mean by a pattern interrupt?

We're all driven by our neurological patterns. For example, children who are attacked by a dog will grow up with a built-in fear of that particular type of dog or any dog that shows aggressive behavior. This is a natural response that gets hardwired into the nervous system. If we can somehow get some input into the nervous system to disrupt that hardwired pattern, it gives the brain the chance to bring itself back into balance and bring itself into more ideal situations.

So, are you saying sickness, disease and pain is a neurological pattern, and the adjustment reboots the brain, and disrupts the pattern, so the body can go back into a state of balance and homeostasis? Yes, that's exactly what it does. The sad thing about the whole situation is we have been so focused on pain reduction as the greatest benefit of chiropractic that we don't ever address the hard issues of the hardwired patterns. We don't see people long enough or often enough over a prolonged period of time to be able to give the brain a real chance to get itself back into a healthy, balanced state.

We need to devise a way of examining the patient's neurological needs, so we can then use whatever technique we deem appropriate for their individual needs.

You suggested earlier that chiropractic was bigger than the subluxation, that it is about brain function, interrupting the patterns, allowing the body to heal. Can you talk a bit more about the fact that subluxation is important, but chiropractic is bigger than that?

Vertebral subluxation exists. I am certainly not saying it doesn't exist. We know misalignments and fixations of the spine occur, but they occur as a tertiary response. The secondary response is more about the muscles that cause the jamming or the fixation that occurs. The primary response is what I call the true subluxation, which takes place in the brain.

We have started to recognize it is the function of the nervous system that creates the distortions, and once you have the distortion in place, you're going to have sensory challenges going on. But, of course, it all started with the brain first, with the starting structure causing more stress at the sensory level.

When I was in chiropractic school, we were taught that the cause of ill health was the subluxation. What you're suggesting, and I think you're absolutely right, is that the subluxation is the effect of a brain and nervous system being out of balance. When the brain goes out of balance, the body does too, not the other way around. Of course we still have to correct the subluxation because it creates the pattern interrupt to help the brain go back into balance.

Interestingly enough, Stevenson says it's all in the brain. He claims it's not the vertebral subluxation at all that's the problem. It's the brain where the problem lies. We, as chiropractors, missed that. It's so easy to jump on board with vertebral subluxation being the cause because it's where it was originally thought to be. The problem is that after more than a hundred years, it still remains a theory. It's never been proven. We chiropractors have to move faster. We need to bring ourselves up to date with neuroscience if, as a profession, we are going to continue to exist.

If we can get on board with the neuroscience and realize we don't have to forsake any of our philosophy to do it, then we can build this profession back up to being in the primary field of healthcare. The bottom line is we deal directly with the nervous system. Every time you give an adjustment, you are directly affecting the function of the central nervous system. This puts us in the role of Functional Neurology.

Most doctors don't realize posture is nothing more than a neurological program.

Your posture is a picture of your dyskinesia. Your abnormal neurological pattern is reflected in your posture and your emotions.

I have had the pleasure and the honor of coaching many Neuroinfiniti neurologically-based chiropractic doctors and one of the things I always focus on with them is language skills. How to keep it simple and talk at a level the ordinary person on the street can understand, rather than trying to blind them with technical terminology. I always try to reduce it down to the simplest of terms such as all stress causes brain imbalance, brain imbalance causes body imbalance. The adjustment reboots and resets the brain and when the brain is balanced the body will balance itself accordingly.

I always refer to the sympathetic nervous system as our survival nervous system, and the parasympathetic nervous system as our healing nervous system. If one is in survival mode, then the other cannot be healing. They have to be in balance to work with each other.

Your care plan is obviously based around the malfunction of the central nervous system, the damage or trauma to the nervous system and how the brain is out of balance. Could you tell us a bit about how you form a foundation for care plans?

There are three things that are important in a care plan. How often we're going to see the patient and how long we're going to be seeing them are obviously the two best-known aspects of the care plan. The third is one that is never taken into consideration. It is the intensity of the care. When your patient is in an over-aroused state, you don't want to be doing a lot of intense work. This can make the problem worse. It may be we have to see them twice per week over a longer period of time doing light work such as cranial-sacral, because we would be dealing with the parasympathetic. It's based on patient need.

You've mentioned intensity, frequency and duration. Can we just focus on intensity?

Intensity can also refer to the number of visits in a week or the number of areas adjusted in any one session. So intensity involves technique, as we said, but it also refers to how often, the frequency of the treatments and the number of areas being dealt with.

So just to sum up, to make sure our readers are on the same page here, you and I believe in lifetime chiropractic care. The question we're asking right now is how often, how many regions and how frequently should we be adjusting our patients, and with what force? We're not saying they need a certain amount of care and then they're done. They are going to need care and to be checked for the rest of their lives to maintain the balance we want to achieve. As chiropractic is built around the central nervous system, and the central nervous system is constantly under stress and constantly having to adapt to stress, then it's going to need attention for the rest of our lives. Is this what you're saying?

Absolutely. All you have to do is recognize the world doesn't stop. The stress isn't going to stop either. The initial goal is to get them out of the danger they're in when they first come to the practice. We want to get them stabilized. Then the goal becomes one of keeping them at their ideal performance for as long as we possibly can.

My background is in Neurology and Rehabilitation, focusing on the hemispheric imbalance. As chiropractors we're always looking at the imbalances and postures, imbalances and muscle tone, and how a person usually has pain on one side of the body or another, and we have imbalance in the postural system. This can lead to imbalances in the vestibular system, the eyes, and the active emotional system. We then realized this was reflective and/or could cause an imbalance in the brain itself where one hemisphere could become stronger than the other. These weaknesses in the brain can start to influence every other system in the body so you can see the imbalances in the autonomic system, the immune system, the brain and cognitive function as well.

A Conversation
with Rob Melillo, DC

My background is in Neurology and Rehabilitation, focusing on hemispheric imbalance. As chiropractors, we're always looking at the imbalances and postures, imbalances and muscle tone and how a person usually has pain on one side of the body or another. When we have imbalance in the postural system, this can lead to imbalances in the vestibular system, the eyes, and the active emotion system. We then realized this was reflective and/or could cause an imbalance in the brain itself where one hemisphere could become stronger than the other. These weaknesses in the brain can start to influence every other system in the body, and you could begin to see imbalances in the autonomic system, the immune system, the brain and cognitive function as well.

When I asked pediatricians, pediatric neurologists or anybody else I thought would know about ADHD, they had no idea what it was, what caused it, or what was going on inside the brain. There was little research on it at all. It was a virtual unknown.

Over the years we've seen a real increase in the number of children diagnosed with ADHD. I went out and spoke to teachers about this to see whether I was just diagnosing it more or if there truly was an increase in the number of cases. What I found was there truly was an increase in the number of cases, and teachers were noticing it more and more in their pupils.

One of the teachers I spoke to recommended a book called 'Endangered Minds' written by Jane Healy. Jane was a PhD in Education for 30 years. She is an expert in the field and her book, published in 1992, showed there was a true increase in the number of cases of ADHD to epidemic proportions.

It wasn't until I went to a conference on ADHD run by the National Institute of Mental Health that I began to realize there was a real hemispheric relationship going on. In fact, the head of the conference pointed out that whatever was happening in ADHD also seemed to be happening in Autism, Dyslexia, OCD and Tourette's. In fact, around 80 percent of the children diagnosed with ADHD also have OCD and Tourette's.

I eventually put together enough research on the subject that I was able to write a book called "Neurobehavioral Disorders of Childhood: An Evolutionary Perspective." While I was researching and writing this book, I came up with the concept of the hemispheric imbalance we're talking about today and the term "functional disconnection" where the two hemispheres of the brain are functionally disconnected. What I didn't realize at the time was that Dr. Jerry Lisman, someone I had been corresponding with on the subject, had already come up with the same terms years before.

We joined together and worked to form an actual research institute looking at what we were now referring to as "functional neurology," which is the science behind the chiropractic rehabilitation and Brain-Based Wellness we're dealing with now. We're not talking about lesions on the brain or anything like that, but functional imbalances within the nervous system.

I wrote a second book in 2009 called "Disconnected Kids," which was the essence of the hemispheric program I've developed. I have been teaching and using this program in my own practice as well. I wanted to put it out there for parents and teachers to be able to use and practice alongside the doctors. Even today, it is still one of the best selling books on Amazon. I wrote a sequel in 2011 called "Reconnected Kids." Then this year I published a further book on the subject trying to go deeper into what causes all of these problems entitled "Autism: The Scientific Truth About Preventing, Diagnosing and Treating Autism Spectrum Disorders and What Parents Can Do Now."

Using this information
in your own practice

When we're looking at a subluxation—a subluxation being defined as an imbalance in muscle tone that creates a juxtaposition relationship in the spine, disrupting the biomechanics—this can lead to degeneration and lead to all of the problems we have already been discussing. What is reflective of an imbalance of this kind is an imbalance in muscle tone, which can be a reflection of an imbalance in the nervous system and the brain.

When D.D. Palmer adjusted Harvey Lillard, causing him to regain his hearing, he achieved it not through the adjusting of the nerves in the spine but by changing the balance and tone of the brain by adjusting the muscle tone of the spine. When you're able to hear something you weren't able to hear before, it's not because there is a change in your muscles, but rather because there is a change in your brain. Changes to the muscles in the body have the greatest effect on the brain. By creating a balance in the body, you can create a balance in the brain. By creating balance in the brain, you're also creating balance in the immune system.

If for whatever reason you're carrying an imbalance in the

brain, then to some extent you're also going to have an imbalance in all of your other systems within the body. This means for the average chiropractor, when you're adjusting someone, they are not only going to see relief from pain and changes in muscle tone, but they are also going to see improved balance and coordination. There are going to be changes in their immune response, changes in heart rate and rhythm, changes in breathing, sexual function, hormone function and their ability to detoxify.

The other thing that is important to understand is when you're dealing with imbalances in the body is you may need to be more specific. What I mean by this is you may need to think about doing an adjustment on one side or the other, rather than just doing a general adjustment.

Thinking within chiropractic has shifted enormously over recent years. Previously, chiropractors were trained to think about adjusting subluxations to relieve pressure in the nervous system. In reality, we are learning now that we are, in fact, adjusting subluxations to normalize and maximize brain function. This is a significant leap in our thinking and I think it elevates the chiropractic field significantly once people begin to understand it.

Anatomy of the brain

We know through evolution that brain development only came about when living creatures started to move. Motor activity was the impetus to developing a brain and nervous system. Once you start to move in a purposeful way, you have to make a decision. You need to either be moving towards something or away from it. Right off the bat, there is a dichotomy. There is a split in the nervous system. One part of the nervous system will drive us towards something and the other will drive us away. Right from the start, from the first creature that was able to move, there was a split in the nervous system and the brain.

Everyone in this field understands that movement is what created the brain originally and it is what creates the brain in every single human being. We're all born with certain primitive reflexes that allow us to interact with our world from the moment we enter it—the primary one being of movement.

In fact, we're all born with just 25 percent of our full brain. As we start to move and interact with the world, more and more we get feedback from our senses, which stimulate genes, causing our brain cells to grow. By our third year, we have around 90 percent of our brains. This massive growth is all due to the fact that we move within and interact with the world around us.

We can start to see problems developing with the symmetry of a child's motor system from an early age. If they have problems with suckling or breastfeeding, low muscle tone, or they can't roll over at three to five months, for example, we know there is an asymmetry in their motor system. Since they don't have a fully developed brain yet, and we know the motor system is what drives the sensory system, and is ultimately going to drive the development of the brain, then right away we're going to see an imbalance developing in the brain as well.

Further, we know both sides of the brain develop at different stages. The right side of the brain begins to develop most in the first two or three years, followed by the left side of the brain. If we don't catch the imbalance early on, it's going to lead to an imbalance in the way the brain develops. This is then going to lead to awkward movements, poor coordination, low muscle tone, and imbalance in muscle tone, ultimately leading to a subluxation or an imbalance of the muscles in the spine.

Imbalances in the muscles of the spine lead to altered feedback or an imbalance of the feedback to the brain, ultimately altering the activity and the development of the brain. If this imbalance in the brain is too great, then the right and the left side can't coordinate properly. They can't share information and you end up with what we call a "functional disconnection." This disconnection between the halves of the brain is the leading theory as to the causes of Autism, ADHD, OCD, Tourette's and Schizophrenia.

So what we see as chiropractors is that you assess the motor system and the sensory system by looking at the patient's muscle tone, posture, and head tilt. You can see if someone has a subluxation. You can determine whether one side of the brain is underdeveloped and then you can change the muscle tone accordingly. Of course, you're going to be improving the balance, coordination and muscle tone of the body. But then at the same time you've also changed the coordination, tone and communication in the brain.

You're also going to see that once you balance the brain out, the immune system also comes into balance. We're also going to see the sympathetic and the parasympathetic nervous systems become more balanced. This has tremendous effects on the person, the body and the overall health and wellbeing of the patient.

Every adjustment that you're going to make to the spine is going to create a shift in the brain function. But of course there are always ways to make the adjustments more powerful and effective, simply by understanding the information we have been talking about here. As we said, it's a paradigm shift in understanding and knowing that what we do as chiropractors affects brain function.

In fact as D.D. Palmer said in his book The Chiropractor, "Chiropractic was founded on tone," which is consistent with everything we've been discussing throughout. We could talk about the tone of the motor system and the tone of the sensory nervous system. It's all about tone and restoring the proper tone to the body and the brain. Again, as chiropractors, we have both a curse and a blessing. The blessing is that even administered improperly, the results can be great, but when done properly we are unstoppable.

I think a lot of people have avoided research because they're afraid that in some way it's going to discredit what we do as chiropractors when in fact it's quite the opposite. The more we go into the research, the more it validates what we do. People should embrace research and use it to help support chiropractic, because it's the only way we're going to get fully recognized.

CHAPTER

ELEVEN

Brain Based Wellness
and the 21st Century Chiropractor

Brain Based Wellness
and the 21st Century Chiropractor

In this chapter, we going to present a number of different strategies relating to brain-wellness, neurologically-based chiropractic, and implementation.

We will cover specific types of adjustments, natural antidotes to stress, becoming less insurance dependent and marketing and advertising; as well as giving you some specific action steps to take.

The initial reasoning behind this book was to create a new conversation for the chiropractic practice. We believe it's time to move away from only relieving nerve pressure and into incorporating and maximizing brain function. It's a pivotal and transformational place for doctors of chiropractic to be. We recognize it can be a difficult place to be as well, because it's difficult to move from doing what you've always done into something new.

Dr. Jeff Camper, an instructor at Logan Chiropractic College says, "We are brain doctors and we affect brain function through the chiropractic adjustment."

We are excited and proud to say this idea is catching fire. This concept makes a lot of sense and is producing amazing clinical results. The most important benefit of this is it gets people more engaged in their practice. Quite frankly, it's pivotal that doctors learn a new language, a new conversation and new habits if they want to run a successful and thriving practice in today's world.

The Brain-Based Wellness concept has been in development since the 1980s, and its time has now come. We truly believe Brain-Based Wellness is a natural fit with what we've been doing all along as chiropractors—working with the brain and nervous system.

Chiropractors have always been open to what makes a holistic change in the individual, so we believe this is a perfect time to turn the focus towards Brain Based Wellness, rather than just focusing on the adjustment side of the equation.

Chiropractic has been a long and incredible journey, but one that we practitioners have enjoyed immensely. Now, however, it is evident that we must make some changes to our practices, and open up to what's going on out there in the world.

As we go into more detail about this, it's important to remember that we are in the most stressful time in human history. We live in such a fast-paced, high-tech world that people are being bombarded with stress all the time. We are all being barraged with more stress than we even realize, with things like electromagnetic frequencies affecting our brains and nervous systems without us even being aware of it.

Physical stress, chemical stress, and emotional stress all translate into brain stress. And when the brain is stressed, it goes out of balance. Unfortunately, when the brain is out of balance, the body always follows. This is what creates sickness and disease. The good news is as we reboot, re-harmonize, and normalize the brain, the body follows and starts to heal, repair and regenerate back to normalcy.

So many people today are stressed past capacity and are in sympathetic overload. They've been stuck in Sympathetic Survival Syndrome for so long that chiropractic adjustment often is not enough. This is why we're introducing the MindFit system to work in conjunction with specific and neurologically-based chiropractic adjustments.

We have seen astounding results with the combination of chiropractic and Brain-Based Wellness. It's the most powerful and effective two-part antidote to stress we've come across in thirty-five years of chiropractic and, to our knowledge, there is no better way to create balance symmetry, harmony, healing, and health.

People have every right to feel however they want to feel. Our job is to educate them—to help them understand that feeling lousy is not normal. We also must convince them that if they don't change their belief systems or retrain their brains, nothing is going to change. Without brain balance, you'll keep doing what you're doing and feeling the way you're feeling.

If you've been dulling the blade because you've been exposed to too much stress for too long, it is vital you shake things up by doing the right type of brain entrainment. This is what we specialize in with the MindFit Neuro-Trainer.

There's a big difference between just taking a nap and having a session using the MindFit system. When somebody goes to sleep on their own, they're not changing anything. They're staying in the same thinking and way of doing things. When you start to challenge the brain through what we call Strategic Mind-Messaging, you start challenging old beliefs and liberating the mind.

Brain-Based Wellness from the chiropractic perspective

One of the most important things we have ever taught our clients is learning how to put themselves in a peak state. People exist in either a peak state or a weak state. We've all experienced peak performance for short spans of time. It comes and goes. It's fleeting and it seems to be outside of our control. Unfortunately, most of us spend more time in a weak state where your words are wrong, your actions don't work and you feel like you're walking on eggshells.

The truth is we are all capable of being in a peak state whenever we want. There are three things everybody can do to intentionally get into a peak state—even without the benefit of the MindFit.

First, you must change their breathing. You must oxygenate the brain, and can do so easily by breathing in through your nose deeply and out through your mouth from the diaphragm. When we breathe we should be breathing out two times longer than the time it takes for us to breathe in because inhalation stimulates the sympathetic system and exhalation stimulates the parasympathetic system. So first we're calming down and oxygenating the brain while putting ourselves into a more relaxed state.

The second thing we have to do to be in a peak state is change our physiology. We have to change our posture. No one would deny standing is a more powerful posture than sitting; and sitting up straight is a more powerful posture than slumping or lying down. When we're moving with intention and confidence, we feel more powerful than standing still. A change in physiology stimulates proprioception and brain function.

The third thing we have to do to put ourselves into a peak state is focus on what we want. This is a difficult step for most people. Most people aren't even aware of what they want. They are very aware of what they don't want, but when it comes to expressing real wants and desires they are at a loss. To be at peak, we need to learn to focus on our desired outcome, whatever that may be.

Part of the secret to putting someone in a peak state is a good adjustment. One of the first visible signs you have normalized and are able to maximize brain function following a specific and corrective chiropractic adjustment is noticing when the patient takes a deep sigh. This will be unconscious on their part as they oxygenate the brain and change the sympathetic-parasympathetic balance.

After the adjustment, you should notice when the patient stands up, bears weight and starts to move, they are now in a better posture, moving differently, and once again stimulating brain function. As the doctor, you should ask them to take a few steps and tell you what is working better, compared to the pain they were experiencing before.

Are they breathing easier? Is posture improved? Are they moving with less stress?

Are your eyes clearer? Are you more energized and awake?

These are quick and easy signs that you've put someone in a peak state. The patient will look at us relaxed, peaceful and happy. That's someone in a peak state.

We know the MindFit system puts people into a peak state as well as a proper adjustment. From a chiropractic perspective, we know 20 percent creates 80 percent of the results. What we mean by that is that 20 percent of the twenty- four vertebrae create 80 percent of the results you consistently produce. No one, regardless of the technique, would argue against the fact that the occipital-atlanto-axial articulation is the most important vertebra in the entire spine for many reasons. Neurologically, physiologically—this is it. This is the area where we de-stress and reboot the brain most frequently and dramatically.

There are a couple of other critical areas. For example, one of the things that as a chiropractor you know is that the greatest percentage of emotional stress in the nervous system ends up subluxating the fifth thoracic vertebra. This is an important fact. When you have someone who's stressed, if you just gently adjust T5, you should feel the release and hear the sympathetic sigh from the patient.

We are also aware that we have to have our sacrum balanced. This is the foundation and it's also responsible for the pump of the cerebro-spinal fluid. It's involved with respiration. When we're stressed, we tend to hold our breath and the sacrum tends to lock up, so we have to make sure the sacrum is moving properly.

It's important to note most subluxations caused by emotional stress can be found from the mid-dorsal up to the occiput, and those subluxations caused by physical stress will usually be found from the mid-dorsal down to the sacrum.

We also focus on areas such as C5 and C6 and T8 and T10. These are the 20 percent key vertebrae that you want to primarily focus on. If you were ever in a situation where you didn't do an evaluation on a patient—which, of course, we don't recommend—regardless of their age or condition, you could pick one, two or three vertebrae to adjust within the key ones and get good results. When it comes to adjusting remember less is more.

Adjusting fewer vertebrae is much better than trying to adjust seven, ten or fifteen. If you were restricted, you'd probably look at the sacrum, T5, and atlas as the go-to areas without even doing the evaluation.

In addition to these areas, there are other things for us to consider. For example, part of the breakthrough we learned from Dr. Richard Barwell is the concept of frequency, duration, and intensity. How frequently do we adjust the patient? How many segments should we adjust? The level of force is determined by what's going on with brain function based on stress level.

These are all key considerations. Barwell taught us there are four primary dysfunctions in the brain. It is over-aroused, under-aroused, unstable or exhausted. Each of these dysfunctions produces different clinical problems and requires a different frequency, duration and intensity when you adjust.

There is a huge new movement in chiropractic to adjust only one side of the patient versus both sides, based on brain imbalance. This is called unilateral adjusting to stimulate the dysfunctional side of the brain. To do this, the chiropractor will study someone's eye orbits—not the actual eyeball, but the orbit. When someone is stressed and their brain is out of balance, one of their eye orbits is going to be more almond shaped and the other would be bigger and rounder.

The almond-shaped side shows you where the brain is not functioning as well, where it's out of balance. Then you would know you need to adjust the other side. We want to stimulate one side of the brain, not necessarily both. One of the reasons some chiropractors get stuck is because they're either adjusting too many segments or they're adjusting both sides of the spine or they're not aware of the frequency, duration, and intensity equation.

These are three extremely important advancements in chiropractic care and adjusting that have all come about from neurologic evaluations in the last few years. As more doctors of chiropractic become aware of and apply these new concepts, the profession will be able to heal more and more patients. This is all part of the importance of chiropractors understanding this conversation, understanding the ramifications of stress and how it affects the entire body, and understanding the whole consciousness of creating Brain-Based Wellness through chiropractic care—and especially through chiropractic care in addition to the MindFit system.

In brain science, it's well known that when the body is under stress, part of our brain literally shuts down. What we mean by this is one of the two sides of the brain, right or left, will cease to function properly when under stress. To test this theory, stand up and balance on one foot. Do a circle in the air with the raised foot. Once you've got your balance and can do the circle, use a finger to write your name in the air. The goal is to attempt to write your name in the air and complete the circle at the same time.

You're going to find that you are unable to do both at the same time. For instance, if you don't remember how to spell your name because you're doing the circle, it means your right brain is dominant and your creative brain is more in control. If you found you could write your name but the circle started to go analog, which meant it started to kick out like you're keeping the rhythm to the music, you're probably more left brain dominant.

That tells us you need to train the two brains to work together and work on doing more whole-brain exercises. That's what the Mind-Fit is designed to do. You can also do things like martial arts, play a musical instrument, or do yoga. These are all whole brain activities. So what chiropractors are realizing is people tend to use one side of their brain more than the other. The side that needs to be worked on is the dormant side, because when you're under stressful situations your most powerful ally—your brain—is shutting down. If we can learn to keep it active, balanced and working, imagine how much better we can think, act and respond in stressful situations when clear thinking is needed most.

As experienced chiropractors, I'm sure you've all faced a situation wherein a patient has a particular issue, you adjust them, and they seem to get better. All of a sudden, on the next visit, the problem is much worse. The reason is because we're not balancing the brain. We're over stimulating the side that is already over stimulated and not stimulating the side that is under stimulated. So clearly, knowing which side to adjust, how often to adjust, and with what intensity to adjust is part of the magic formula in addition to knowing which vertebra to adjust. If doctors of chiropractic can become more aware of this and begin incorporating the MindFit system into their practices, they would begin seeing amazing sustainable clinical results and would develop the reputation to which we all aspire. When our confidence goes up, new patient attraction goes up, retention goes up and everything improves. This is the target to which we should all be aiming.

Generating income

Our professionals have spent a lot of time devising and testing ways to diversify income streams for you and assist you in moving away from insurance dependence. With new health care changes in the works, there is no sure way of knowing how each independent doctor will be affected by the changes. One thing that's certain is it's getting harder and harder to work effectively within the constraints of the insurance industry. Moving away from dependence on insurance for income streams is a smart move.

One of the many benefits of the MindFit system is it's a cash-based system. It's based on the value it creates. It allows us to make significant amounts of money helping people, without actual chiropractic doctors being forced to spend much time and effort on the system because it's basically run by the staff in your office.

The first thing you need to understand is people will pay cash for this service without it being dependent on insurance companies. They're going to pay someone for something similar anyway. Why shouldn't it be you?

For example, we don't have to tell you that the weight loss industry has been growing by the billions since the mid-1990s. People will continue to eat processed foods and continue to become overweight and obese. And they are willing to pay just about any amount of money in their attempt to find a solution to the weight loss problem. By adding weight loss, you can easily add $15,000 a month or more to your practice with very little effort—and that doesn't include all the other programs that are possible with this system. The sky is the limit, but you have to have a plan.

We have over 600 clinics now in the United States using the Brain-Based Wellness solution. Currently we are gathering information from all of those clinics and using it to advise our doctors. This is a relatively new business. Few people have capitalized on it yet.

Almost a trillion dollars was spent on alternative care between 2010 and 2011. People are willing to spend the money and there's no better market than the chiropractors who have the space to turn their locations into a Chiro-Spa. People want to be taken care of physically, mentally and emotionally. You've been doing a great job physically, now it's time to step it up in the mental and emotional side of things and capitalize on that.

Implementation

One of the most important things necessary in the implementation phase is using a proven system. Instead of flying by the seat of your pants or making it up as you go along, it's vitally important that you have a plan. You have to have a system. Once you get them in the chair, it's easy to put the headphones and glasses on and press play. That's not complicated at all, but a lot of work, training and planning goes into getting them into the chair.

It's important to be firm with your patients. Too many chiropractors ask bad questions such as "Would you like to try this?" Or "Can you afford this?"

This program needs to be presented as a big part of their overall wellness program. Doctors make recommendations for patient care all the time. This should be no different.

What we train our doctors to do is say to their patient, "You're now at the phase of care where we need to move to the next level. In addition to your ongoing chiropractic care, I recommend you try our new Brain-Based Wellness. I'm going to give you a free demonstration today. If during this twenty-minute pain-free relaxation session you fall asleep or find yourself feeling relaxed, centered and peaceful or perhaps even focused and energized, feeling great, then we can consider this a positive test. You will thrive from this new recommendation for your care. So have a seat, lie back and relax and when you're done we'll see if you have any or all of these responses."

As we've explained to you previously, we already know that between 98 and 99 percent of people are going to have an amazing experience and want to know more about what you're offering. So then we go over it. This is a twelve-week program. It takes the average adult twelve weeks to create new connections in their brains. We have found that two sessions per week is ideal.

Then we'd go over the fees for the program. If the person is a current patient, you might want to reduce the fee for 24 sessions to $50 a session or $1000 for the program. If it's an entirely new client, we generally charge $1200 but would include chiropractic consultation, history and exam in order to convert a MindFit client into adding chiropractic care.

Marketing and advertising

You want to proceed with caution with advertising until you learn what works and what doesn't work within your market.
The main thing is to start the conversation in your office and let current patients know what's going on. Pick out your ten to twenty top patients, and get their feedback. Get them to tell you how well this is going to work.

Once you have your buzz created, go ahead and print some flyers with your doctor's picture and pick a date for a seminar or client event. There's no reason any chiropractor wouldn't be able to get ten or twenty of their most active patients to help them fill a hotel room with a hundred people. We have had offices that were able to bring in five hundred people. Once you have your top patients secured, your staff should begin handing flyers to anyone who comes in the office.

During that event or seminar, you offer each and every person the chance to come in and experience a free demo session. You have ready-made people that have heard the story, who know about the solution, and they can then start to appreciate how the technology is going to help them de-stress and make the changes they want in their lives.

Remember, you as the doctor and your staff need to set aside time to experience this system every day yourselves. It's important for you to have experienced what you're trying to sell to your patients.

Create a plan for your patients including what topics you're going to cover, where you're going to implement, what you're going to charge for it, how you're going to market and promote it and, once you're rolling, how to increase your client base.

Final message

The final message we want to give you is we are here available to help. Stay in touch with us. You can contact Dr. Bob Hoffman at bob@themastercircle.com, or contact Dr. Patrick Porter at patrick@portervision.com. Feel free to ask your questions. Take progressive action steps. Gain confidence. Make it work and you will produce better clinical results and drive your profitability.

The most important point you can take away from this is we have to be better chiropractors. We've got to continue to refine our skills, make better distinctions, and help people get over stress and over their illnesses faster and more efficiently. The combination of great chiropractic care and the MindFit system does all this and more.

This has been an amazing journey and, quite frankly, we've just begun.

CHAPTER
TWELVE

Additional Resources

Dr. Patrick Porter's
Stress-Free Lifestyle Series

Stress is the most pervasive malady of our time. The effects on our health, productivity and quality of life are more devastating than most people care to admit. Luckily, you've just found the solution! CVR can help you see yourself as the healthy, happy, optimistic person you'd prefer to be. With this new image, your fears and frustrations fade away, your anxiety vanishes, and you no longer let small things stress you.

Create Your Enchanted Forest for Stress Reduction

Follow along as Dr. Patrick Porter guides you through your personal enchanted forest—a quiet, serene place where you have nothing to do but relax. Your other-than-conscious mind will massage away all tension, allowing you to release all negative thoughts and feelings. You'll return from your magical forest filled with positive feelings, able to enjoy and express your true inner peace.

Create Your Mountaintop Retreat for Stress Reduction

Say goodbye to all stress and confusion as you take a trip to this breathtaking mountaintop retreat. When you listen to this restful process, using your mind to relax your body will become as comfortable and automatic as breathing. The stress, strain and confusion of everyday life will melt away as you awake refreshed, revitalized and renewed!

A Complete List of
Stress-Free Titles
and full descriptions
can be found at
www.YourFlourishingBrain.com/SMT

Dr. Patrick Porter's
Vibrant Health Series

Of all the cells in your body, more than 50,000 will die and be replaced with new cells, all in the time it took you to read this sentence! Your body is the vehicle you have been given for the journey of your life. How you treat your body determines how it will treat you. Taking good care of your body will go a long way in ensuring that your life is active, happy, and full of positive experiences. Dr. Patrick Porter will show you how, by using creative visualization and relaxation (CVR), you can recharge and energize your body, mind, and spirit. This series is for people who are looking for more than good health; it's for those who will settle for nothing less than vibrant health!

Staying Focused in the Present
Your emotions can either help your body stay healthy, or they can be the cause of disease. Negative feelings such as regret, worry, or anxiety about an upcoming event not only wastes your precious life, but also adds stress to the body, which makes you more susceptible to disease. In this CVR process, Dr. Porter will help you stay present and focused on the beauty of each moment and the gift each minute offers you.

Visualize a Heart-Healthy Lifestyle
Heart disease is not a male issue alone; it is the top killer of American women. To protect your heart, you need a plan that includes movement, a healthy diet, and a positive mental attitude. You use an average of forty-three muscles to frown and only seventeen muscles to smile. You'll find smiling even easier now that you are taking an active roll in protecting the health of your heart. During this CVR session, Dr. Porter will show you how to celebrate the energy, passion, and power that are your birthright.

Check Out The Complete
Vibrant Health Series
at www.YourFlourishingBrain.com/SMT

Dr. Patrick Porter's
Life-Mastery Series

Throughout your life, from parents, teachers, and society, you were taught what to think. With the breakthrough processes of creative visualization and relaxation, you are going to discover how to think. With this knowledge you will literally become a software engineer for your own mind. On the Life-Mastery journey, you will explore the processes that best suit your needs for creating limitless personal improvement and success in your life.

Ask, Believe & Receive
Visualization
The universe operates on specific laws. These invisible laws are always manifesting your physical reality. The universe never tries anything; it only does. This visualization calls upon the Law of Attraction, and helps you to become a conscious creator. You will discover how you designed, at the core of your being, to be an active participant in the enfoldment of your relationships, wealth and happiness.

The Secret Power of Self-talk
On average, you give yourself over 5,000 messages a day. With this process you will discover how to weed your mental garden of negative thoughts and to sow new, more positive thoughts. You will use the same four-step process that has helped thousands of people neutralize fear, anxiety and worry. Using CVR, you discover the secret power of self-talk to easily create the habits, patterns, and beliefs that can put your success on autopilot.

Check Out The Complete
Life-Mastery Series
at www.YourFlourishingBrain.com/SMT

Dr. Patrick Porter's
Wealth Consciousness Series

Inspired by the principles of Napoleon Hill's Think and Grow Rich

Start Each Day with Purpose and Passion

Napoleon Hill understood that people don't plan to fail; they fail to plan. Successful people know where they are going before they start and move forward on their own initiative. They have the power of intention, or what Napoleon Hill called "mind energy," on their side. Dr. Patrick Porter (PhD) will guide you in using this power of intention to focus your imagination on the success and prosperity you desire.

Commit to a Life Spent with Like-Minded People

Together with Dr. Patrick Porter, you will use the power of intention to draw to yourself mastermind alliances that will support your dream. You will visualize setting up and using these mastermind alliances to help you attract goal-oriented people and create your success environment.

Trust the Power of Infinite Intelligence

Do you sometimes feel as though negative thoughts and fear of poverty have control over you? During this CVR session, Dr. Porter will guide you through the principle of applied faith. All conditions are the off-spring of thought, and you find it natural to visualize and realize the thoughts and actions that bring wealth and riches into your life.

Check Out The Complete
Wealth Consciousness Series
at www.YourFlourishingBrain.com/SMT

Dr. Patrick Porter's
Weight Control Series

Now you can design the body you want and the life you love. That's right, you can have the trim, healthy body you've always dreamed

of by simply changing the way you see yourself and your life. Once you have a new image of yourself, everything else changes—junk food and fast food lose their appeal, healthy foods become desirable, and you eat only when you're hungry. With Dr. Porter's System you will overcome common weight loss mistakes, learn to eat and think like a naturally thin person, conquer cravings, and increase your self-confidence. Each week you will take another step toward a lifetime of healthy living; losing weight is the natural byproduct of these changes. While the average diet lasts just 72 hours and focuses on depriving you of the foods you love, Dr. Patrick Porter supercharges your weight loss motivation with these powerful creative visualization and relaxation processes! You will eliminate the problem where it started—your own mind. There is simply no easier way to lose weight than CVR!

Safely Speeding Up Weight Loss
In this powerful process, you'll learn to safely speed up weight loss by thinking, acting and responding like a naturally thin person. Your sense of worth will improve when you discover and use inner resources you never even knew you had. Sit back, relax, and discover how easy it is to turn your body into a fat-burning machine—and keep the weight off forever!

Check Out The Complete
Weight Control Series
at www.YourFlourishingBrain.com/SMT

Dr. Patrick Porter's
Accelerated Learning Series

Whether you are an honor student or just having difficulty taking a test, this breakthrough learning system will help you overcome learning challenges and accelerate your current skill level. Imagine doubling your reading speed while improving your memory. Sit back, relax and allow your mind to organize your life, while you build your self-confidence and earn better grades with the our complete learning system.

Setting Goals for Learning Success
Dr. Porter's Pikeville College study proved that the more successful students are those who have an outcome or ultimate goal in mind. With this module you will learn the secrets of goal setting, experience a boost in motivation, and see your self-confidence in the classroom soar.

Being an Optimistic Thinker
Henry Ford once said, "Whether you think you can, or you think you can't, you are right." It all starts with attitude. You will be guided into the creative state, where you'll discover ways of breaking through to your optimistic mind that will help you to think, act and respond with a positive nature even during your most difficult classes or around challenging people.

Six Steps to Using Your Perfect Memory
Harness the natural byproduct of relaxing your mind by using the six steps that activate a perfect memory. You will discover creative ways to access and recall the information you need as you need it! Best of all, you will have this ability the rest of your life.

Check Out The Complete
Accelerated Learning Series
at **www.YourFlourishingBrain.com/SMT**

Dr. Patrick Porter's
HeartDr. Patrick Porter's
Pain-Free Lifestyle Series

Persistent pain can have a costly impact on your life. It can lead to depression, loss of appetite, irritability, anger, loss of sleep, withdrawal from social interaction, and an inability to cope. Fortunately, with creative visualization and relaxation (CVR), pain can almost always be controlled. CVR helps you eliminate pain while you relax, revitalize, and rejuvenate. You deserve to be free of your pain—and now you can be, thanks to CVR!

Tapping into a Pain-Free Lifestyle

Dr. Patrick Porter will guide you through a simple exercise to transform pain into relaxation. You'll tap into your body's innate ability to heal itself, allowing the healing process to happen while you take a relaxing mental vacation. Pain will lose all power over you as you learn to relax away your pain and enjoy your life free from discomfort.

Activate Your Mental Pharmacy
In this dynamic process, you'll unlock your body's natural pharmacy, flushing pain from your body and neutralizing all discomfort. You will so galvanize your mind's healing capacity, all you'll have to do is say the word to release pain, fear and anxiety. Most importantly, you'll have this healing power at your fingertips—when and where you need it most.

Starting the Day Pain-Free
In this motivational session, Dr. Patrick Porter will show you that living pain-free is as simple as saying, "So-Hum." Which means, transporting yourself to a pain-free state can be as easy as breathing! You'll be able to bury your pain in the past and awaken each morning pain-free.

Check Out The Complete
Pain-Free Lifestyle Series
at **www.YourFlourishingBrain.com/SMT**

Dr. Patrick Porter's
Freedom From Addiction Series

Addiction comes in many forms, but the underlying cause remains the same. For every addiction there is an underlying positive intention that the mind is trying to fulfill. Now you can use the power of your mind—through creative visualization and relaxation (CVR)—to find more appropriate ways to satisfy that positive intention without the destructive behaviors of the past. Dr. Patrick Porter's groundbreaking CVR program for overcoming addiction can work   for just about any addiction including the   fol-lowing:

Alcoholism
Anorexia & Bulimia
Codependency
Gambling
Marijuana
Narcotics
Prescription Drugs
Overeating
Overspending
Pornography
Self-Injury
Sexual Promiscuity

Personal Responsibility —Working With Your Other-Than-Conscious Mind to Manage Your Life
Most people who struggle with addictions have, in reality, simply lost their power of choice. Dr. Patrick Porter (PhD) will help you discover why trying to force a change with willpower only perpetuates the problem and how visualization is what will lead you to realization and freedom. You will discover how, by tapping into the power of your mind, you can rebuild your confidence (even in uncertain times) and bring into your consciousness (with sufficient force) the appropriate memories and choices that will lead you to living an addiction-free life—which is your birthright.

Check Out The Complete
Freedom From Addiction Series
at **www.YourFlourishingBrain.com/SMT**

Dr. Patrick Porter's
Coping with Cancer Series

Being diagnosed with cancer is in itself a stressful event—so stressful it can suppress your immune system and worsen the side-effects of treatment. Fortunately, through guided relaxation, you can let go

of your fear and anxiety, and take charge of your recovery. Creative visualization can help you regain an optimistic attitude, spark your immune system, and maximize your medical treatment. If you are ready to join the ranks of people who have discovered the mind/body connection and its healing potential, then the Coping with Cancer Series is definitely for you!

Relaxation For Inner Healing

For some people, relaxing while facing a serious illness may seem like an impossible task. In this first session, you will begin by simply clearing your mind of all negative or fear-based thoughts concerning your condition. At the same time, you will learn to allow the natural healing power of your body to take over. The benefits from relaxation are immeasurable when it comes to fighting cancer.

Rejuvenate Your Body Through Deep Delta Sleep

During cancer recovery, many people have difficulty falling asleep or they may awaken in the middle of the night and struggle to get back to sleep. Your body naturally recharges and rejuvenates during sleep, which means a good night's rest is key to your recovery. This imagery will show you new ways to get maximum benefit from sleep.

Check Out The Complete
Coping With Cancer Series
at **www.YourFlourishingBrain.com/SMT**

Dr. Patrick Porter's
SportZone™ Series

Success in sports is about being the best you can be, and visualization plays a key role in getting there. Why is visualization so important? Because you get what you rehearse in life, but that's not always what you want or intend. This is especially true when you are facing the pressures of athletics. The SportZone program is designed to help you tap into the mind's potential and make your sport of choice fun and enjoyable while taking your game to the next level. Visualization for sports performance is nothing new to top competitors—athletes from Tiger Woods to diver Greg Louganis and a variety of Olympians have used visualization to bring about optimal performance, overcome self-doubt, and give themselves a seemingly unfair advantage over their competition. Now the SportZone series can work for any athlete, from junior competitors to weekend enthusiasts. Yes, you can get more out of your sport and, in the process, get more out of life.

Using the "Zone" in Your Sport
When competitive athletes slip into their "zone" everything seems to work just right. Dr. Patrick Porter will help you get to that place where everything comes together. With this process you'll learn to put yourself into a state of "flow," your own personal "zone," so you can stay on top of your game. The "zone" is as easy to access as a deep breath once you have mastered the mental keys.

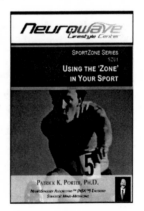

Control Your Emotions and Master Your Sport
It has been said that he or she who angers you conquers you; this is true even if the person who angers you is you! With this process you will learn a powerful self-visualization technique for keeping your emotions under control. With this easy technique you will no longer be giving away your power to others and will stop letting anger and frustration get the better of you.

Check Out The Complete
SportZone Series
at www.YourFlourishingBrain.com/SMT

Dr. Patrick Porter's
Smoking Cessation Series

Kicking your smoking habit doesn't get any easier or more fun than this! When you use Dr. Patrick Porter's proven strategies, you'll find that making this life-saving change comes about simply and effortlessly. With the new science of creative visualization and relaxation (CVR), you will extinguish the stress and frustration associated with quitting smoking, and you'll conquer your cravings like the tens of thousands of others who have used Dr. Porter's processes.

Making the Decision To Be A Non-Smoker

With this CVR session, you'll learn about the cleansing power of you own mind, and use it to take a "mental shower" that will wipe away all thoughts of tobacco. With this process, you'll gladly make the decision to be tobacco-free for life!

Making Peace With Your Mind

In this powerful creative session, Dr. Patrick Porter will show you that, while you once had a positive intention for having tobacco in your life, you no longer need it to live the life you desire. The smoker of the past will make peace with the clean air breather of the future in order to create a new, vibrant you!

Plan Your Life As A Non-Smoker

Every goal needs a plan, and in this process, Dr. Patrick Porter will guide you in visualizing and working a plan for your tobacco-free life. This motivational session will allow you to remember to forget cigarettes forever. You'll awake convinced being a nonsmoker is as easy as taking a breath of fresh air!

Check Out The Complete
Smoking Cessation Series
at www.YourFlourishingBrain.com/SMT

Dr. Patrick Porter's
Mental Coaching for Golf Series

Efficient golfers know how to relax and let their minds take over. Now, thanks to these creative visualization and relaxation (CVR) processes, you'll learn to see yourself as a calm, confident golfer. You deserve to take pleasure in your time on the course. Thanks to CVR, you'll finally be able to let go of frustration and focus on every stroke—meaning you'll not only play better, but you'll also enjoy the game more than ever!

Optimize the Risk Zone for Golf

You've never experienced a practice session like this one! Follow along with Dr. Patrick Porter as he guides you onto the driving range in your mind. Once there, you'll practice each swing, letting go of negative thoughts and allowing the clubs to do what they were designed to do—send the ball straight to the target.

Develop the Attitude of a Champion

Champions understand that good outcomes come from good shots. With this dynamic process, you'll find it easy to think positive thoughts and accept each shot as it comes. You'll no longer spend time feeling distracted, over-analyzing your game, blaming the conditions of the course, or getting angry over a bad lie.

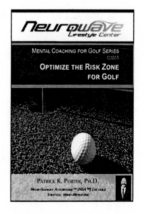

Concentration:
Your Key To Consistency

Most golf professionals consider concentration to be the key to playing golf...but almost no one teaches it. In this energizing process by Dr. Patrick Porter, he'll teach you to achieve the concentration you need simply by sitting back, relaxing, and letting go of all stress and confusion.

Check Out The Complete
Mental Coaching for Golf Series
at www.YourFlourishingBrain.com/SMT

Dr. Patrick Porter's
Enlightened Children's Series

Seven-year-old Marina Mulac and five-year-old Morgan Mulac, who have come to be known as the world's youngest marketers, were the

inspiration behind this Enlightened Children's Series. When they met Dr. Patrick Porter, they had one question for him: Why had he created so many great visualizations for grown ups and nothing for kids?

Dr. Porter told the two little entrepreneurs that if they put on their thinking caps and helped him design a program for kids, together they could help children from around the globe to use their imaginative minds to become better people and help improve the world. Together, Marina, Morgan, and Dr. Patrick Porter put together this series that uses guided imagery, storytelling, and positive affirmations to help children see the world as a peaceful and harmonious place where everyone can win. If your goal is to develop a happy, healthy child of influence in our rapidly changing world, this series is a must-have for your child.

Building Optimism in Your Children
Every day your child is forming his or her view of the world based on life experiences. Now is the time to help your child build a positive outlook that will serve him or her for a lifetime. Optimists believe that people and events are inherently good and that most situations work out for the best. Dr. Porter will show your child how to see the good in every situation and how to be open to experiencing new things.

Check Out The Complete
Enlightened Children's Series
at **www.YourFlourishingBrain.com/SMT**

Brain-Based Wellness

Join Drs. Bob Hoffman and Patrick Porter for an 8-hour, 8-module boot camp that will teach you how to transform your practice from bone to brain quickly, easily & profitably... The Brain-Based Wellness Cash Practice!
Price: $299.00

Price: $299.00

How Experts Deliver
World Class Patient Education

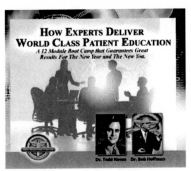

This 12-hour program will teach you the absolute fundamental steps necessary to effectively educate, empower and engage your patients so they consistently choose on-going chiropractic care.
With Drs. Bob Hoffman
and Tedd Koren
Price: $299

The Secrets to Creating
Unlimited LIfetime Chiropractic Patients

This amazing 12-hour, 12-module boot camp will appeal to all doctors of chiropractic, at a fraction of the cost of just one new patient! With Drs. Bob Hoffman and Richard Barwell.

Price: $299.00

The Tools of Mastery

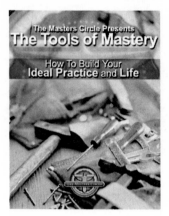

Nine amazing and practical hours of cutting-edge material to show you the exact step-by-step plan to build your ideal practice and life. Learn how to optimize your practice and produce the miracles chiropractic is famous for. Secrets to creating unlimited lifetime chiro patients.
Price: $299

Reader's Discount – Save over 60% on All Four!

Unlock the profits in your practice with this Your Flourishing Brain special promotion. For a modest investment, you can get all four of the above life-changing, practice-building profit proven workshops.

Price: Only $499 (Regularly $1,196 — You save $697!

Email Bob to order at bob@themasterscircle.com

The Masters Circle App helps you stay inspired and grow your practice!

Download *The Masters Circle App* to your smart phone or tablet by searching for it in the app store on your device, or scanning the QR codes below to link directly to the download area.

For our Members, we offer the full array of benefits you're accustomed to in the Member's Area of our website, now conveniently available from within the app.

Features Include:
- About Us Section
- Member's Area
- Free Practice Evaluation
- Upcoming Seminar Schedule & Information
- Upcoming TeleClass, Webinar & Bootcamp Schedules & Information
- TMCtv (Over 200 hours of chiropractic & success videos for TMC members & subscribers)
- TMCtunes (Audio segments on various topics in chiropractic & success for all to enjoy)
- News Letters and Practice Tips
- TMC Daily Blog
- Facebook, Twitter & YouTube Integration
- Success Journal
- TMC Store Access
- DC Locator
- Fan Wall, Fan Cam & Photo Gallery
- Email Signup
- Message Center to Review Recent Push Notifications
- Built in QR Code Scanner
- Share App with Friends & Colleagues Easily
- Learn How to Customize an App Just for Your Practice!
- Links to Important Chiropractic Resources

Important note - This app is brand new, so if you have any questions or problems, before posting a bad review, please email jeremy@themasterscircle.com for quick personalized assistance and we will resolve all issues with a smile.

Please check back regularly for updates, improvements and additional content.

Thank you for your support and engagement in our mission to preserve and advance the chiropractic profession!

Scan this code below with your smart phone to download The Masters Circle App:

Apple

Android

Mastering The Message

Here's What You Will Learn

1. The Seven Timeless Virtues of Successful Communication:

These seven powerful concepts will guide you toward communicating like the masters do – with certainty, conviction, relevance and love.

2. The Ten Essential Elements of the Report of Findings:

Learn how to get patients to commit to their own wellbeing by showing them how making such a commitment suits their ultimate needs.

3. Six Tools To Improve Your Presentation Skills:

Turbo-charge your talks by putting these advanced speaking skills in your toolbox, and watch your patients respond as you weave them into your presentations.

4. Giving The Ultimate Health Care Class:

Hear how an expert engages a chiropractic audience and moves them toward better health and better compliance.

5. The Best Way To Educate Your Patients:

People can grasp your concepts better if you choose simple language and give them a bit of information at a time. This system will streamline and simplify the process so your patients understand.

6. The Five Love Languages and Action Plans For your Growth:

Tap into a chiropractic application of a best-selling book and recognize the different ways you can influence your patients and prospective patients, based on their preferred method of communication.

A $295 Value for FREE!!

Please note, you will receive the six hours of "Mastering the Message" as an audio file.

Go to www.masteredmessage.com to download your free audiofile

The Re-invention of Chiropractic Coaching

What would practice and life be like a few months from now if you had all the new patients you needed and wanted, your compliance and retention transformed to world class status, and you were able to generate far more profit than ever before? Would an extra $2000, $5000 or $10,000 or more each month reduce your stress, increase your happiness and make your confidence soar? The Masters Circle has re-invented chiropractic coaching and our unique approach differs from the other coaching and consulting companies in that we concentrate on helping you improve you - so that your practice follows suit. We have discovered that your personal growth always precedes your practice growth. Just like every man, woman and child would bene fit from lifetime chiropractic care, every Doctor of Chiropractic can benefit from on-going expert coaching.

In 2013, the average coaching member at The Masters Circle grew over 30% - and this number includes new graduates, those in practice over thirty years and struggling, and everything you can imagine in between. Could you benefit from a 10 to 1 return on your investment and become better person in the process?

They say that timing is everything. This is your time to take action. Yes, there are always distractions and projects that you are working on … just another reason why a coach is so necessary right now–to help you be organized, more efficient and totally focused on the projects and actions that truly matter for outstanding and sustainable growth. Let's schedule a call to speak and let us help you fulfill your dreams.

"Since joining The Masters Circle 6 years ago, I've had increased clinical results, increased patient volume and increased income each year. More importantly, after 30 plus years, practice is more fun than ever before. I wish I had joined The Masters Circle years ago, where chiropractic is kept alive and well. The Masters Circle is a wonderful home for both new and established practitioners."

Dr. Tom Salmon, DC

New Jersey

"I joined The Masters Circle 10 years ago, directly out of Chiropractic College. I went to a TMC seminar and was blown away with the congruency and the passion. In addition, the concept of coaching resonated with me. I then put into motion all of the wonderful things my Masters Circle coach told me to do when starting my practice. The systems and strategies that I learned gave me a wonderful foundation for growth and they are still in place today. The Masters Circle has changed my life for the better in every way possible as well as my practice growth and continued success."

Dr. Jared Leon, DC

New York

Give us a call at 800-451-4514 to schedule your complimentary 30 minute practice evaluation.

Please visit www.JoinThe MastersCircle.com or email us at MVP@TheMastersCircle.com

Your Practice Is Your Business...Helping You Grow It Is Ours!

Welcome to The Gift of Love Project

The Gift of Love is a poetic writing that has its own beauty ... and upon further examination, it may lead one to a contemplative process, creating balance and harmony in one's everyday life. Over time, this process can also create subtle positive change in the recipient of **The Gift**.

My guidance leads me to distribute this writing to one billion people within the next two years. Hopefully, many people will be led to practice the contemplative process. If **The Gift of Love** resonates with you, please share it with others. As we gather and hold the **power of love** in our consciousness, we will dramatically reduce the level of anger, fear, and hatred on our planet today. -- Jerry DeShazo

The Gift of Love

*I Agree Today
To Be The Gift of Love.*

*I Agree to Feel Deeply
Love for Others
Independent of Anything
They Are Expressing,
Saying, Doing, or Being.*

*I Agree to Allow Love
As I Know It
To Embrace My Whole Body
And Then to Just Send It
To Them Silently and Secretly.*

*I Agree to Feel it, Accept it, Breathe It
Into Every Cell of My Body on Each In-Breath
And On Each Out-Breath
Exhale Any Feeling Unlike Love.*

*I Will Repeat This Breathing Process Multiple Times
Until I Feel it Fully and Completely
Then Consciously Amplify In Me
The Feeling of Love and Project It to Others
As The Gift of Love.*

*This is My Secret Agreement –
No One Else Is To Know it.*

*This page may be reproduced in totality
for any peaceful purpose without financial gain.
All rights reserved, Jerome DeShazo, D.D., M.B.A.,M.C.C.*

For more about The Gift of Love Project and to view the videos, please visit www. TheGiftofLove.com. You will also be given access to a special 9-minute Creative Visualization that will align you with the **Power of Love** and supercharge your day. Together we will change the world one person at a time.

2014

SEMINAR SCHEDULE

We are proud to announce our 2014 Masters Circle Seminar schedule so that you can select the dates and locations that work best for you and then plan to attend by marking those dates off in your calendar. We consistently find that those members that attend our seminars each year are those members who engage deeper, learn more, implement better and as a result see the most progress and profitability in their practices.

We are asking you to plan to attend our seminars in 2014 so that we can best serve you. It is our intent to share our technology, distinctions, core principles and standards of excellence in the most interactive and most engaging way possible with you and your team.

In addition to your coaching, our seminars are always interactive, information-rich and inspiring. Our seminars are designed to recharge you, renew your confidence and remind you of your purpose and passion. We look forward to growing together with you and your team in 2014.

February 6-8 :: Winners Circle Weekend

March 7-8 :: London Seminar

March 28-29 :: Chicago Seminar

April 4-5 :: NY/NJ Seminar

June 5-7 :: SuperConference in Chicago

September 12-13 :: London Seminar

October 9-11 :: Winners Circle Weekend

November 7-8 :: NY/NJ Seminar

THE MASTERS CIRCLE
YOUR ACCELERATOR FOR SUCCESS

WWW.THEMASTERSCIRCLE.COM | 800.451.4514

Dates and locations are subject to change

CPSIA information can be obtained
at www.ICGtesting.com
Printed in the USA
FSOW01n1520110914
3108FS